THE ROUTLEDGE

HISTORICAL ATLAS

OF

RELIGION

IN

AMERICA

Routledge Atlases of American History

Series Editor: Mark C. Carnes

THE ROUTLEDGE
HISTORICAL ATLAS
OF
RELIGION
IN
AMERICA

BRET E. CARROLL

MARK C. CARNES, SERIES EDITOR

ROUTLEDGE

NEW YORK AND LONDON

Published in 2000 by
Routledge
29 West 35th Street
New York, NY 10001-2299

Published in Great Britain in 2000 by
Routledge
11 New Fetter Lane
London EC4P 4EE

10 9 8 7 6 5 4 3 2 1

Library of Congress Cataloging-in-Publication Data

Carroll, Bret E., 1961–
      The Routledge historical atlas of religion in America / Bret E. Carroll.
          p. cm. — (Routledge atlases of American history)
      Includes bibliographical references and index.
      ISBN 0-415-92131-7 (hardback : alk. Paper) — ISBN 0-415-921137-6 (pbk : alk. Paper)
      1. Ecclesiastical geography—United States—Maps. 2. United States—Church history—Maps.
      3. United States—Religion—Maps. I. Title: Historical atlas of religion in America.
      II. Title. III. Series.

G1201.E4 C3 2000
200'.973'022—dc21

                                                                              00--030007 00059192

To Gilbert Carroll (1926–1973), Judith, and Iris

Contents

Foreword

As the first Americans wandered into North America from Siberia, across frozen wastes that are now severed by the Bering Strait, they sought guidance about the spirit world from their shamans. John Winthrop regarded the safe passage of the Puritans from England to Massachusetts Bay as proof that God had given them "a special commission" to carry out His plans in the New World. Brigham Young viewed the Mormon "great trek" from Nauvoo, Illinois, to the Great Salt Lake Basin as comparable to the exodus of the Hebrews. During the 2000 presidential campaign, Republican George W. Bush named Jesus as his favorite philosopher and declared June 10 "Jesus Day" in Texas. As if in reply, Democratic candidate Al Gore highlighted the fact that Joseph Lieberman, a practicing Jew, shared Gore's belief in "God Almighty." This is to observe that the history of America is inseparable from the history of religion in America. An historical atlas of religion in America reveals much about the history of the American people.

But what is an historical atlas of religion? Most historical atlases, including those in the Routledge series, examine phenomena of a physical character: the construction of railroads, canals, factories; the voluntary or forced migration of peoples—immigrants, Native Americans, slaves; the advance of explorers or the collision of armies. Such activities were geographical in character: for instance moving foodstuffs from the farms of the Midwest to the urban markets in the East; shifting slaves from the exhausted soils of Virginia to the new cotton fields in Mississippi; finding a northwest passage to the Pacific or cutting the Confederacy in two. And because these activities have an explicit geographical dimension, they are easily mapped.

But how does one map ideas about God?

Most atlases avoid this perplexity by equating religion with the institutions of religion. This allows the mapmakers to exploit masses of data on the major religions. These atlases can readily be identified by their ubiquitous dots: some maps depict individual churches, so that the reader will see clusters of green "Catholic" dots in urban New York and blue "Baptist" dots in South Carolina, and smatterings of brown "Jewish" dots for synagogues; other maps, similarly colored, have dots that signify religiously affiliated universities or missions. Much of this familiar data appears in this atlas as well.

But historian Bret E. Carroll is interested in religion as religion—ideas about God and the nature of belief. He makes use of information on religious institutions in order to illuminate patterns of thought and behavior. He seeks to map the pathways of belief in the American past.

Because new religious ideas were often spawned by solitary religious visionaries or preachers, Carroll at times focuses on such individuals. He thus maps the efforts of Indian prophets of revitalization, ranging from the prophet Popé, who inspired the Pueblo revolt against the Spanish in 1680, to the Paiute visionary, Wovoka, whose transformation of the "Ghost Dance" alarmed whites and resulted in the massacre of Indians at Wounded Knee in 1890. Carroll shows the routes of celebrated preachers such as George Whitefield during the First

Great Awakening of the 1730s and 1740s and of Charles Grandison Finney during the Second Great Awakening a century later. He also depicts activities as varied as the founding of Indian villages by the Puritan missionary John Eliot, the establishment of the Oneidan communes by John Humphrey Noyes, and the blending of eastern and western thought in the Theosophy of the Russian emigrant, Helena Blavatsky.

Carroll understands, further, that religious ideas were spread by groups of people as well as individual preachers or prophets. He locates the multiple origins of American Lutheranism in Sweden, the German Palatinate, and the Netherlands, and tracks its passage, respectively, to the Delaware Valley, the Carolinas, and New York. He shows the origins and merging of voodoo traditions, "call-and-response" worship, and Christian hymnody among slaves.

Carroll devotes considerable attention to missions, which were often central to the transmission of religious ideas. In addition to the usual accounts of Spanish missionaries in the South and French Jesuits along the upper Mississippi and Great Lakes, Carroll describes the diffusion of Russian Orthodox missions in Alaska and the Northwest, Protestant missionary activities in India and China throughout the 19th century, and even the AME Zion (African-American Protestant) missions to Africa during the last third of the 19th century.

Historical atlases that concentrate on religious institutions contain a built-in bias in favor of the major denominations, which, by virtue of their size and continuity, have generated and preserved the information on which such atlases depend. By treating such matters succinctly, Carroll has reserved far more space to consider the full diversity of religious belief and practice in America. Thus his atlas alone includes maps of such extraordinary range as Eskimo bear rites of neolithic times, the 18th-century migration of the Jews from 17th-century Holland and Brazil, the evolution of the Disciples of Christ in the trans-Appalachian West, the origin and spread of Christian Science, the rise of Malcolm X and the Nation of Islam, and the development of a host of 20th-century faiths ranging from Zen Buddhism, Protestant fundamentalism, Pentecostalism, the Unification Church of Sun Myung Moon, the Scientology of science fiction writer L. Ron Hubbard, and the syncretic Baha'i.

Tocqueville was struck by the dull pragmatism of the American people, whose contributions to philosophy, literature, and the arts were, he maintained, modest indeed. But he was impressed that so materialistic a people could succumb to such extravagant religious views and passions. Carroll makes a strong case that religion is the field in which American thought has attained its greatest creativity. He has managed to capture the eye-popping splendor of this imaginative profusion. We must stare hard at it all, for if we cannot understand its religious beliefs, we cannot understand the American nation.

Mark C. Carnes
Barnard College, Columbia University

Introduction

American religious life, like American culture more generally, is nothing if not colorful. From the outset, it has been multiform, diverse, protean, and dynamic. This is what makes its study so interesting. But its kaleidoscopic nature is perhaps better represented by a crazy quilt than by a mandala—there is no single overall pattern—a fact which presents daunting challenges to anyone who would attempt to understand and explain it, and particularly to those who would do so through cartographic or other visual images. Nor is its almost bewildering diversity the only challenge to the student or teacher of American religion. Religion is in important ways—perhaps its *most* important way—a personal thing that is only partially expressed in outward behaviors and institutions and defies analysis, measurement, and quantification. Ultimately, mapping human spirituality may well be impossible. The user of this atlas ought to approach it—as did the author—with these provisos in mind.

But this atlas is predicated on the belief that there is a story—or, perhaps more accurately, many stories, many small patterns rather than one large one—that can be conveyed through maps. Such central themes as migration, immigration, geographic expansion, regional concentration, and the formation of institutions and communities *are* amenable to cartographic expression. Using these overarching themes, this atlas attempts to provide an introductory overview of American religious history, highlighting the rich and colorful diversity that has characterized it since the first peopling of what is now the United States some tens of thousands of years ago. To grasp this diversity is to grasp one of the basic—some would say defining—features of American life. Indeed, because the United States is a land of immigrants and has thereby become home to most of the world's religions, an appreciation of American diversity may lead to an appreciation of the nation's cultural sources in and interrelationships with other regions of the globe.

Diversity has become an important organizing—and disorganizing—principle in studies of American religion, past and present. Not long ago, the nation's religious history was understood in terms of white Protestant domination and development: beginning with English Puritans, white Protestants of European background moved westward starting in the 17th century, first across the Atlantic and then across the North American continent, creating and defining a religious "mainstream." But scholars have increasingly sought in recent years a new historical understanding, a "decentered" approach that removes white Protestants from the heart of the story and challenges the very idea of a "mainstream" to represent more completely and accurately the complexity of America's religious past. Geographically, this new approach has involved a recognition that the conventionally emphasized east-to-west developmental trajectory of white Euro-American Protestantism has coexisted with equally significant west-to-east and south-to-north movements, usually by nonwhite and/or non-Protestant peoples and religions from places other than Europe, across the Pacific Ocean and Bering Sea as well as the Atlantic, and in many cases long before the arrival of the Puritans. This atlas is intended to reflect this "state of the art." It presents a textual and cartographic portrait of the nation's religious diversity and multidirectionality, devoting space to groups and geographic movements traditionally slighted and first bringing Protestantism into view only in the third part.

While this atlas is devoted above all to conveying the diversity of American religious experience, its size does not permit the inclusion or full coverage of all of the thousands of groups and movements that populate U.S. religious history. Its method is to divide that history into six chronologically and topically defined periods, successive but overlapping, and to examine and map the major new developments in each. Groups and movements that exist across long stretches of time arise, therefore, only at moments of particular historical importance. Thus, for example, the Baptists appear only periodically: in the chapter on the colonial period, when they first arrived on the American scene; in the chapter on the 19th century, when waves of revivalism propelled them to their status as the nation's largest Protestant denomination; and in the chapter on modern America, when they contributed to and benefited from a resurgence of conservative evangelical Protestantism in American life.

Native American religions are treated in the first part, for the history of religion in America begins with them. The second and third parts examine European colonization and settlement in North America, first by non-English Europeans from the 16th through the 19th centuries and then by the English in the 17th and 18th centuries. With these groups came the many Judeo-Christian traditions, and particularly the Protestant ones, that gradually and sometimes coercively came to dominate, if never entirely to define, American religious culture. Part four explores the Protestant expansion, innovation, and experimentation, among both white and black Americans, that framed 19th-century American religious life. The fifth part, covering the period from about 1850 to the present, examines the immigration of peoples and religions from Eastern Europe, Asia, the Middle East, and Latin America. Arriving especially from 1880 to 1920 and again after World War II, they transformed America's Protestant diversity into a diversity far more inclusive. Part six focuses on the 20th century, when the forces shaping modern American life—urbanization, industrialization, technology, continuing immigration, and internationalism— elicited religious responses and produced new movements that expanded American religion in all of its dimensions. An epilogue examining American religious regions—geographic areas defined by the particular religious characteristics of their residents—is intended to summarize the whole and to examine what is perhaps the most important concept used by geographers and historians to map American religious diversity and discern some order in its apparent chaos.

While this atlas cannot completely span the breadth and plumb the depth of American religious history, it can introduce the rich tapestry of religious impulses and expressions so central to the American and human experiences. The reader is welcomed to a fascinating world.

PART I: INDIGENOUS AMERICAN RELIGIONS, PREHISTORY–PRESENT

American religious history began some 30,000 to 50,000 years ago when, according to archaeologists, the first human beings set foot on the North American continent. An Ice Age expansion of the Arctic ice cap reduced sea levels sufficiently to expose an area of land currently submerged beneath the Bering Sea and called Beringia. This tundra region attracted eastward-moving hunters from northeastern Siberia, who brought with them their Paleolithic Asiatic cultures and belief systems.

The Beringian crossing ended when milder climatic conditions and rising sea levels obliterated the land bridge, perhaps 10,000 years ago. By then the descendants of the Siberian migrants had spread over the tundra, grasslands, deserts, plateaus, and forests of the Americas, adapting to a wide range of environments and developing their Paleolithic religiosity into a correspondingly wide variety of forms. Meanwhile, Indonesian, Micronesian, and Melanesian peoples of south Asian origin carried other Paleolithic religious forms eastward across the Pacific Ocean to the islands of Polynesia and, by about 500 CE, northward from Tahiti and the Marquesas Islands to the

This Southeastern shell gorget from about 1000 CE depicts a shaman, suggesting the retention of Northern hunting traditions in Southern agricultural religious practice.

Hawaiian Islands. By the time of European colonization, about 75 million people inhabited the Americas, perhaps 10 million of them in what is now the United States. They were divided into hundreds of ethnic groups, spoke hundreds of languages, practiced an array of subsistence techniques, developed many different patterns of social organization, interacted with each other through trade, migration, and warfare, and devised a kaleidoscopic range of religious systems to address the circumstances of existence. In shaping and reshaping their religions in response to experiences of migration, adaptation, and intercultural exchange, they established enduring patterns of American religious life.

This diversity complicates any attempt to present indigenous American religions in general terms, but historians and anthropologists have identified several broad characteristics and constructed models by which to make sense of their variety. Perhaps the most basic point about Amerindian religion is that those behaviors and attitudes we term "religious" were for them the central orienting mechanism in a single seamless reality of cosmos, landscape, culture, society, and economy. American aborigines understood themselves as participants in a world of spiritual power at once natural and supernatural—called *Wakan* by the Sioux, *Orenda* by the Iroquois, *Manitou* by the Algonkians, and *Mana* by Hawaiians—upon which they depended for survival and which they encountered mainly through its effects in the natural world. This spiritual force infused humans, animals, plants, landscape features, and natural phenomena and bound them into an integrated web of existence. Humans were only one—and by no means the most powerful—of nature's active powers.

Native Americans expressed such beliefs in their various origin myths, intended to explain cosmically their geographic location, their relationship to

This Shoshone hide painting of a buffalo dance suggests the importance of the buffalo and hunting to ritual life on the Plains.

the environment, and their social and cultural systems. These myths were expressed in rituals, which differed from group to group but aimed through sacred words, songs, gestures, and objects to align humanity with the spiritual world and to harness its powers for personal or group welfare. The assurances of ritual were particularly important at crucial junctures in the life of the group (before and after hunts and wars, for example, or at the time of planting and harvest) or of the individual (puberty, illness, or death). Many groups identified certain individuals, called *shamans* (usually but not always men), as possessing special spiritual gifts that gave them authority to conduct rituals, but most groups also emphasized ordinary people's connection to the spiritual world and encouraged personal ritual encounters with it, as men might do before hunting or women when menstruating.

In addition to such broad commonalities, scholars have identified two broad and interpenetrating "traditions" within North America's precontact indigenous religions. The first was a Paleolithic "northern hunting tradition" that came to the continent with the first Siberians and spread eastward and southward; the other was a younger "southern agrarian tradition" that accompanied the development of settled agricultural economies in Mesoamerica and spread northward with maize cultivation. After contact with white Europeans and Americans, Amerindian groups developed a spectrum of religious responses, often categorized into "revitalization" and "accommodation" movements, by which they resisted or adapted to an expanding Euro-American presence and rethought their relations with the land.

Northern Hunting Religions

Northern hunting religions developed from those of Paleolithic Siberia and Beringia. Their features were evident wherever hunting was common but remained most pronounced in northern North America.

America's hunting peoples regarded animals, on which they depended for survival and which appeared well adapted to environmental conditions, as superior in wisdom and power and deserving of respect and reverence. Their origin myths typically featured local animals as earth's shapers and first inhabitants. Great Lakes tribes, for instance, attributed hills, valleys, and streams to a Great Beaver that dredged soil from a primeval sea and a hawk that flapped its wings to dry it. A Great Hare then summoned human beings into existence and taught them to survive. Many northern tribes were divided into clans claiming descent from animal ancestors.

Hunting and animals dominated ritual life as well. Throughout the Northeast and on the Plains, hunters sought the supernatural aid of bear, eagle, and badger spirits in dramatic vision quests. Shamans conducted collective rites that used imitative gesture and costume to petition desired animals prior to hunting and offered ceremonial thanks to the animal spirits afterward. Arctic Eskimo solemnly addressed Grandfather Bear, while tribes of the Pacific Northwest returned the skeletons of a season's first salmon catch to rivers in order to ensure continued supplies. On the Plains, Sioux, Pawnee, and Osage ritual reflected dependence on buffalo.

The shaman was particularly important in most hunting tribes. Most shamans of the Americas beckoned spirits to approach and possess them, but those of the Arctic, Bering, and north Pacific Coast regions retained the Siberian practice of spirit flight, their souls traveling great distances to contend with powerful spirits and ensure successful hunting. Other groups looked less to shamans than to medicine men or secret societies for healing magic.

Hunting groups dealt gingerly with the female power of fertility, thought harmful to the spiritual power men required for hunting. Tlingit men, for instance, considered continence a prerequisite for prehunt visions, and men of whaling tribes sometimes avoided their wives for the entire whaling season. Menstruating women were ceremonially isolated from the group and forbidden contact with all objects touched by the men. Young women learned of their power in rites of passage at first menses.

Native religions often symbolized environmental hazards as spirits. Many Eskimo peoples, like their Siberian ancestors, feared a cannibal spirit representing what was probably a grim reality of Arctic life. The Ojibwa of the Great Lakes likewise hoped that the cannibal spirit Windigo would not visit in nightmares. Eskimo hunters also imagined a half-human, half-animal spirit that, like the vast whiteness of the landscape, threatened to hypnotize and destroy them. Harmful shouting spirits might bedevil hunters in the cold, windy forests of western Canada and the Pacific Northwest. Such were the challenges, difficulties, and religious expressions of hunting life in the North.

Northern hunting tradition

- Beringia land bridge
- → spread of Northern hunting tradition

bear rites rite

Indian cultures

- West Arctic
- West Sub-Arctic
- Northwest Coast, Upper
- Northwest Coast, Lower
- Central California
- Southern California
- Plateau
- Great Basin, Desert
- Plains Nomad
- Southwest
- East Arctic
- East Sub-Arctic
- Prairie or Plains Village
- Iroquois
- North Atlantic
- Southeast

shaman spirit voyages

bear rites

cannibal spirits

Northern hunting tradition

animal reverence, shamanism, hunting and healing rituals

shaman spirit voyages

salmon spirit voyages

salmon rites

shouting spirits

vision quests
cannibal spirits

earth diver tales

vision quests

vision quests
buffalo rites and dances

vision quests

Victoria Island

Great Bear Lake

Great Slave Lake

Baffin Island

Hudson Bay

Newfoundland

L. Winnipeg

L. Superior
L. Michigan
L. Huron
L. Ontario
L. Erie

St. Lawrence R.

Missouri R.

Colorado R.

Arkansas R.

Mississippi R.

Rio Grande

PACIFIC OCEAN

ATLANTIC OCEAN

Gulf of Mexico

Tropic of Cancer

N

0   400 km
0   400 miles

Southern Agricultural Religions

Maize agriculture, developed in Mesoamerica about 3000 BCE, sparked settled village life, complex social structures, an intensified astronomical and meteor-ological awareness, and characteristic religious patterns in which priesthoods and rich collective rites fostered community bonding and addressed the chal-lenges of agricultural life. Such patterns spread gradually northward into what is now the United States.

Evidence of urban centers and ceremonial burial mounds among the Adena and Hopewell peoples of the Ohio Valley suggests that agricultural religion had reached the region by 1000 BCE. It was more fully devel-oped by the Mississippi Valley civilization, which flourished about 1250 CE, cultivated corn, constructed temple mounds for collective rituals, and centered on the city of Cahokia. This civilization dis-appeared long before Europeans arrived, but it left behind what are now the oldest religious structures on the American landscape and powerfully shaped subsequent cultures in the lower Mississippi Valley.

A Zuni kachina doll. These figures were used by tribes in the desert Southwest to summon rain-bringing spirits.

Planting tribes revered and expressed in myth the power of agriculture. The Hopi and Zuni of the Southwest imagined that their ancestors emerged from holes in the earth (*sipapu*) after Father Sky or Father Sun brought rain to Mother Earth and that they learned to plant corn from Corn Mothers. They conducted many rituals in subterranean *kivas* in recognition of these origins. Southeastern peoples also explained human origins in terms of descent from the sky and understood Father Sun as the source of life.

Agricultural ritual celebrated and sought to control plants, planting, har-vest, rain, and sun. Petitions to Father Sun at summer and winter solstices were common in the Southeast. Cherokee and Creek Green Corn ceremonies and similar rites thanked and perpetuated seasonal rhythms by sacrificing the "first fruits" of important crops. Ceremonial cornmeal offerings likewise character-ized the Southwest. Many Southern tribes considered tobacco a particularly effective means of petition. On the Plains, the hunter-gatherer Pawnees and others smoked it through calumets to honor the Corn Mother and the Keeper of Buffalo. In the Southwest, where rain was rare, the Hopi and Zuni held summer *kiva* rituals and public ceremonies invoking rain-bringing ancestral spirits (*kachinas*) through cornmeal, pollen, and dance. Near the current Mexican border, the Papago and Pima sought rain through song and ritually consumed cactus cider—tribes farther south used corn liquor—every June.

Agricultural religions never ceased resembling the hunter traditions from which they evolved. Indeed, the common roots of the two traditions, the migra-tion of peoples, and variations in physical and cultural environments produced a complex reality in which agricultural and hunting rites were more often than not mixed. The Creeks of Alabama and Georgia, who hunted and planted, retained shamans and hunting rituals alongside their fertility observances. The Iroquois, who migrated northward to New York from the Ohio Valley around 1200 CE, retained Mississippian features rare in the North: complex social organization, a full ceremonial calendar, and a priesthood that conducted rituals for corn, beans, and maple syrup. The Navajo, who migrated southward from the subarctic to the Desert Southwest, combined the visions, healing magic, and cold-weather concerns of Northern hunters with the priests and rain ceremonies more typical of the region. Such systems suggest the dynamism and complexity of pre-Columbian American religion.

Southern agricultural tradition

→ spread of Southern agricultural tradition

CREEK tribe

Mississippian civilization

▨ heartland

◯ primary area of influence

◯ secondary area of influence (dashed)

● main temple mound

Indian cultures

West Arctic

West Sub-Arctic

Northwest Coast, Upper

Northwest Coast, Lower

Central California

Southern California

Plateau

Great Basin, Desert

Plains Nomad

Southwest

East Arctic

East Sub-Arctic

Prairie or Plains Village

Iroquois

North Atlantic

Southeast

Ancient Hawaiian Religion

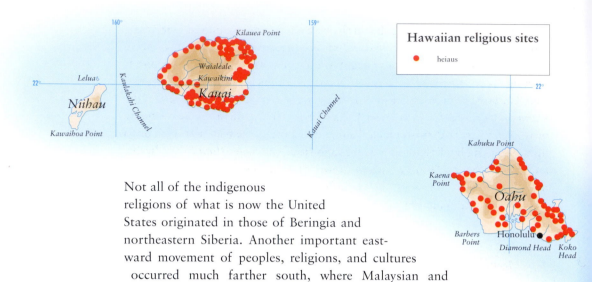

Hawaiian religious sites

● heiaus

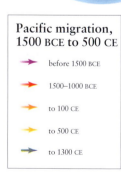

Pacific migration,
1500 BCE to 500 CE

→ before 1500 BCE

→ 1500–1000 BCE

→ to 100 CE

→ to 500 CE

→ to 1300 CE

Not all of the indigenous religions of what is now the United States originated in those of Beringia and northeastern Siberia. Another important eastward movement of peoples, religions, and cultures occurred much farther south, where Malaysian and Indonesian islanders of south Asian descent, driven by adventure, warfare, or a search for food supplies, pushed across the Pacific Ocean, gradually settling first the islands of Micronesia and Melanesia, and then those of Polynesia, including Tahiti, Easter Island, and the Marquesas. Archaeological data suggest that northward oceanic migration had led inhabitants of the Marquesas to Hawaii by around 500 CE—making the islands probably the last in the Pacific to be occupied by human beings—and that larger streams of Tahitians arrived in Hawaii between 900 and 1300 CE. Native Hawaiian religion and language became increasingly distinct over time but show clear similarities to the Tahitian. Hawaiian and Tahitian cultures in turn point to their shared origins in the Asian and oceanic cultures to their west.

Ancient Hawaiian religious belief and practice were much like those of other Paleolithic peoples, emphasizing the spiritual power assumed to underlie every aspect of life, its specific manifestation in various natural forces and places, its exercise by humanized deities of varying functions, and its manipulability at the hands of ritual specialists. More specifically, Hawaiian religion resembled those of other Polynesians, with such powerful geological and geographical realities as the ocean, volcanic activity, and reliance on plants and sea animals figuring prominently. Hawaiians traced everything to the sky father Wakea and the earth mother Papa, including the deities. The most important of these were the creator Kane (like the Tahitian Tane), the storm, rain, and fertility deity Lono, war deity Ku, and Kanaloa (in Tahiti, Ta'aroa), deity of the sea and of death. Lesser deities were associated with vulcanism (Pele), sharks, and canoe building. The Hawaiian supernatural world was also populated by *aumakua* (beings that protected specific families), *unihipili* (spirits of the dead that were able to inhabit other people), and *kapua* (trickster beings capable of changing form).

The power of these beings lay in their ability to control *mana*, a universal force that shaped the world and could move from one person, object, or place to another. Human beings also sought to use *mana* as well for their purposes, looking especially to their priests (*kahunas*), who sought through rituals (also called *kahunas*), often held in particular enclosed areas (*heiaus*), to bring the *mana* of specific deities into carved figures representing them, to use the *mana* of the sea water that surrounded them and seemed to them so powerful, or to induce healing by directing *mana* through ritual massages (*lomilomi*), herbs, and sacred objects. Dealing with the power of *mana* also required observance of taboos (*kapus*) meant to protect either people from *mana* or *mana* from people. Thus chiefs or war leaders maintained their power through certain required or prohibited behaviors, and fishing was disallowed at certain times so that the fish might retain the *mana* necessary to reproduce. Varying *kapus* distinguished the chiefs (*alii*) from others, and the *heiaus*, usually located around the perimeter of an island, were important loci of

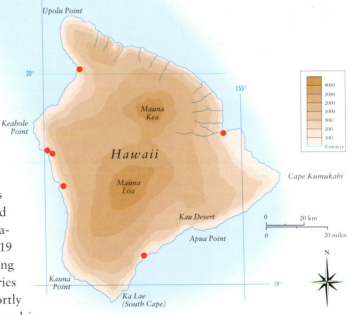

the power they wielded in tandem with the priests. At the same time, Hawaiians considered themselves bound together in a shared existence by a power called *aloha*.

While this aboriginal religion and related social system survived the arrival of Spanish explorers in the 16th century and of Captain James Cook in 1778, the *kapus*, *kahunas*, and *heiaus* were abolished by a new genera-tion of Hawaiian royals after the 1819 death of Kamehameha I, thus facilitating the efforts of the Protestant missionaries who arrived from New England shortly thereafter. But the ancient ways endured in Hawaiian folk culture as Hawaiians continued to respect *mana* and to regard *heiaus* and other locations as sacred places.

Postcontact Revitalization and Accommodation

Contact with Euro-Americans brought indigenous Americans disease, depopulation, physical dislocation, and cultural displacement, triggering among them a variety of religious responses. Some resisted these changes and attempted to revitalize ancestral ways, while others sought to accommodate indigenous traditions to new conditions. Both responses rested heavily on the traditional practice of vision seeking and, often drew on Christianity as well.

As early as 1680, Pueblo shaman Popé urged revitalization and inspired a (temporarily) successful rebellion against Spanish colonizers in New Mexico. By the 18th and 19th centuries, religions of resistance developed in response to westward-moving Anglo-American settlement. In the Ohio Valley, the "Delaware prophet" Neolin sparked Chief Pontiac's 1763 uprising, and "Shawnee prophet" Tenskatawa in turn inspired his brother Tecumseh to lead campaigns between 1805 and 1814. By 1832, "Winnebago prophet" White Cloud inspired Black Hawk's armed resistance movement in the upper Mississippi Valley. These later movements were intertribal, suggesting a growing sense of shared racial and spiritual identity among Indians.

By the late 19th century, such movements became pan-Indian and interregional as continuing Euro-American expansion through the Missouri Valley and on the Pacific coast intensified pressure on Indian lands, food supplies, and cultures. In Washington in the 1850s, Catholic-educated Wanapum shaman Smohalla experienced visions in which earth's original Indian inhabitants lived in Edenic harmony with Mother Earth until later-arriving whites wounded her with metal ploughs. In 1877, Nez Percé Chief Joseph made this ideology the basis for an unsuccessful armed rebellion. The prophet Wodziwob sparked a similar movement among the Paiute of Nevada and California around 1870, teaching in Christian apocalyptic imagery that the earth would swallow humanity but that followers of a special dance would be resurrected into a revitalized world without whites. The dance spread among several Western tribes, then faded for a time.

Paiute prophet Wovoka. His Ghost Dance spread among Native Americans in the late 19th century in response to expanding Euro-American settlement.

In 1889 it was revived and transformed into the "Ghost Dance" by Paiute visionary Wovoka, who combined visions, ritual dance, the reception of supernatural tokens, and Christian eschatology. His followers, much like Wodziwob's, sought through dance to achieve reunion with dead Indians of the past in a renewed prewhite world. The Ghost Dance spread eastward, assuming local variations. The Lakota Sioux, seeking to replenish the disappearing buffalo, modified it to resemble their Sun Dance. The Oglala Sioux added "Ghost Shirts," garments ritually empowered by the dance to repel bullets. The dance aroused misunderstanding and fear among whites, generating tensions that culminated in an 1890 massacre of Indians at Wounded Knee. Though many tribes subsequently abandoned the dance, the Pawnees retained it into the 20th century, and it has sometimes resurfaced amid late-20th-century Indian militancy.

Other movements sought accommodation to white culture. Around 1800, Seneca prophet and visionary Ganiodaio (Handsome Lake) proposed a new way of life called the *Gaiwiio* to an Iroquois population suffering social disintegration. His teachings blended apocalyptic prophecy with a Protestant (particularly Quaker) ethic of peace, temperance, settled agriculture, private land ownership, economic enterprise, and domesticity. Ganiodaio's code proved attractive and continues by some estimates to shape the lives of perhaps one-quarter of reservation Iroquois.

Peyote religion has been another effective accommodation strategy. The ritual ingestion of peyote—a hallucinogenic cactus of southern Texas and northern Mexico—had characterized Mexican agricultural rituals as early as 1000 CE, but its use in the United States dates from around 1870, when the Mescalero Apache of Texas began acquiring it for their shamans. Peyote rituals spread progressively northward, changing as they went. By 1880, the Kiowas, Comanches, and Caddos, confined to reservations in what is now Oklahoma, were using it in their dances, and among the Plains tribes it became itself the focus of ritual. After the demise of the Ghost Dance, and due to the promotional efforts of Delaware-Caddo tribe member John Wilson and Comanche chief Quannah Parker, peyote religion became a particularly appealing means of nonviolent accommodation. Parker blended Christian and indigenous traditions into the "Peyote Way," an ethical system counseling self-discipline and participation in the white economy, and a combinative ritual. The ritual varies from group to group in extent of Christian content, but was loosely formalized in the 1944 establishment of the Native American Church. Peyote religion remains widely practiced, contributing substantially to pan-Indian consciousness despite its multiformity.

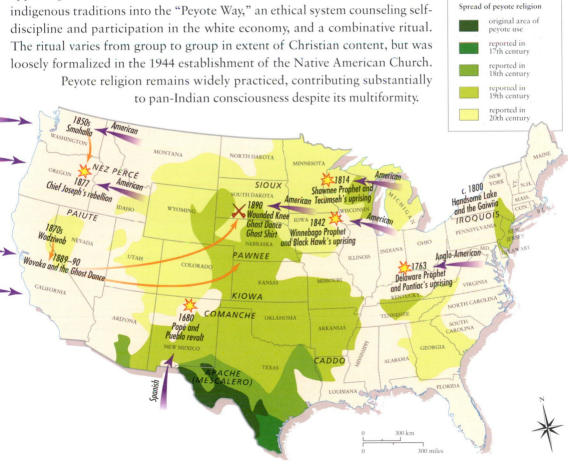

Postcontact religions

SIOUX tribe

European and American pressure responsible for resistance movements

influence

battle

rebellion or uprising

Spread of peyote religion

original area of peyote use

reported in 17th century

reported in 18th century

reported in 19th century

reported in 20th century

1850s Smohalla — American
WASHINGTON
MONTANA
NORTH DAKOTA
MINNESOTA
NEZ PERCE
1877 Chief Joseph's rebellion — American
OREGON
IDAHO
WYOMING
SIOUX
SOUTH DAKOTA
1890 Wounded Knee Ghost Dance Ghost Shirt
American
1814 Shawnee Prophet and Tecumseh's uprising — American
MICHIGAN
WISCONSIN
NEW YORK
VT. N.H.
MASS. CON. R.I.
c. 1800 Handsome Lake and the Gaiwiio
IROQUOIS
PENNSYLVANIA
NEW JERSEY
PAIUTE
1870s Wodziwob
NEVADA
1889–90 Wovoka and the Ghost Dance
UTAH
COLORADO
PAWNEE
IOWA
1842 Winnebago Prophet and Black Hawk's uprising — American
NEBRASKA
ILLINOIS
INDIANA
OHIO
DELAWARE
MD.
Anglo-American
1763 Delaware Prophet and Pontiac's uprising
VIRGINIA
KENTUCKY
CALIFORNIA
KANSAS
MISSOURI
KIOWA
COMANCHE
OKLAHOMA
ARKANSAS
TENNESSEE
NORTH CAROLINA
SOUTH CAROLINA
ARIZONA
1680 Popé and Pueblo revolt
NEW MEXICO
TEXAS
CADDO
MISSISSIPPI
ALABAMA
GEORGIA
Spanish
APACHE (MESCALERO)
LOUISIANA
FLORIDA

0   300 km
0   300 miles

PART II: EUROPEAN CHRISTIANITY COLONIZES AMERICA, 1500–1867

Amongst the sedentary agricultural peoples, like the Pueblo Indians, the Spanish built their missions amongst existing settlements. In this reconstruction of Cicuye, later known as Pecos, the mission was constructed at the southern end of the fortified site.

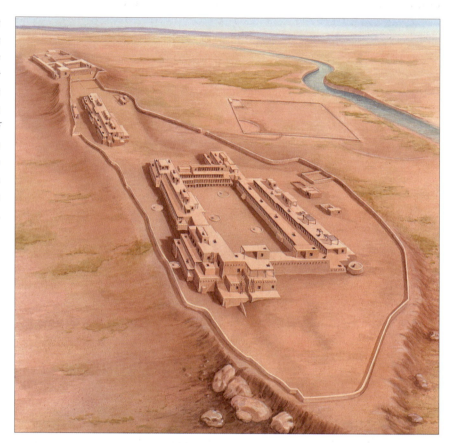

The colonization of the Americas by European peoples between the 15th and 19th centuries, approaching from across the Atlantic Ocean, Pacific Ocean, and Bering Sea, was perhaps the most important transformation in American religious history. Steeped in Christian tradition and driven by missionary zeal, the pursuit of wealth, and geopolitical rivalry, European colonizers—Spanish and French Catholics, Russian Orthodox, and British, Dutch, and Swedish Protestants—undertook to Europeanize and Christianize the American landscape.

Whether and to what extent they and their descendants Christianized America are matters of debate. But their arrival certainly intensified and redefined the dynamic intermixing of peoples, religions, and cultures that indigenous Americans had already established as a constant of American life, and they and their descendants became dominant in a culturally reconstituted America. Religious beliefs and institutions were central to both processes: they were mechanisms of cross-cultural interaction, European cultural imperialism, and what became a massive transformation of the North American continent.

The new Americans operated on very different understandings of space and time indigenous Americans. The latter considered their landscapes from those of timeless, their existence one of perpetual being, but the Europeans imagined a world moving through linear time in accordance with a divine plan discernible in terrestrial events—including their settlement of a "New World." And whereas Amerindians sacralized the natural landscape, Europeans were inclined to separate sacred space from nature and dotted their new environment with religious structures intentionally insulated from it. They also, pursuing what they believed were God's plans for the continent, constructed farms and factories, roads and railroads, and—on a greater scale than had the Indians—towns and cities.

Indians and Europeans also understood each other very differently. Natives tended at first to regard the Europeans in traditional terms: either as peoples like any other, suitable for alliance or rivalry, or as deities with powers that might be harnessed to enhance control of the environment. Their worldviews included little basis for discerning long-term conflicts of interest between peoples, and only as the newcomers' patterns of behavior and settlement became clear did they develop new and racially aware religious expressions addressing the altered realities of American life. The Europeans, on the other hand, understood natives virtually from the start as racially different, and as peoples to be either converted or displaced in pursuit of their religious aspirations for the "New World."

Colonization by Europeans and their religions changed the fundamental premises of American religious life. Their arrival intensified the process of transoceanic migration and the various west-to-east, east-to-west, south-to-north, and north-to-south movements by which the American religious landscape became peopled, developed, and diversified. They sought utterly to transform their new surroundings and understood religious pluralism as a matter of increasing and often anxious concern. Physically and spiritually, they were redefining America.

Ferdinand Deppe's 1832 painting of the mission of San Gabriel, just north of Los Angeles, was made the year before the Mexican government dissolved the mission.

Spanish Catholic Colonization

Spanish Catholics colonized America and its peoples—whom they considered spiritually benighted—with a religious and nationalistic zeal stemming from Spain's 1492 unification and subsequent expulsion of Muslims and Jews. They established a church, diocese, and bishop in Puerto Rico by 1513 and by the 1530s had begun sending Franciscan, Dominican, and Augustinian missionaries—joined later by Jesuits—to Mexico. By the early 19th century, Spain's enormous American empire—New Spain—encompassed what is now the Latin America and, on its northern edge, the southern rim of the United States.

Hampered by distance from Spain and the rest of Mexico, and in desert areas by a forbidding landscape and climate, missionary efforts in northern New Spain were initially meager but increasingly substantial. Along the Florida and Guale (Georgia) coasts, French settlement in 1564 stimulated Spain to found a line of missions from St. Augustine, Florida (1565) to Santa Elena (Port Royal, South Carolina). French activity in the lower Mississippi Valley after the 1670s likewise prompted missionaries to move northward to found missions in the Florida panhandle, and from Mexico to do likewise in eastern Texas. These missions were soon undercut by Indian uprisings in defense of native customs, tense relations with the Spanish government, and,

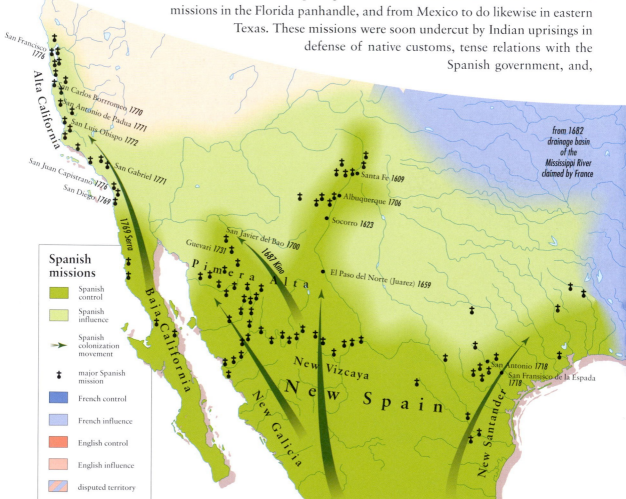

in Texas, geographic isolation. Longer-lived missions appeared in eastern and central Texas during the early 18th century, but English colonization on the Atlantic coast prevented a resurgence in Florida.

Missions in present-day New Mexico and Arizona fared little better. Between 1598 and 1630, Franciscan friars moving northward from Mexico established thirty missions in New Mexico's Rio Grande Valley, but their aggressive methods prompted Pueblo peoples to eject them in the 1680 Pueblo Revolt. Missions reappeared in 1693, diminished in influence but contributing to an enduring creolized culture centered in Santa Fe and blending Catholicism with indigenous religion. Meanwhile, Jesuit Eusebio Francisco Kino (1654–1711) founded several missions in Arizona after moving northward from Sonora in 1687, but these were stifled by Pima Indian revolts in 1751 and 1781 and by the eviction of the Jesuits from the empire in 1768. Franciscans replaced the Jesuits but withdrew in 1828.

In California, Junípero Serra (1713–84) and other Franciscans moved northward from Baja California amid rising Spanish concerns about Russian activity along the north Pacific coast. They established twenty-one missions stretching 600 miles from San Diego to Sonoma (north of San Francisco) between 1769 and 1823. Using benevolent paternalism, a creole language, and occasional harsh punishment, they set up profitable agricultural communities and coaxed more than 21,000 Indians to a European "way of life." But in 1833 the newly independent Mexican government dissolved the missions, sold their lands and buildings, and scattered the Indian communities. Both Spanish Catholic and Native American cultures in California were further eroded by the transfer of California to the United States in 1848 and subsequent influx of diverse American and immigrant groups.

Only with Hispanic immigration in the 20th century, much of it to the nation's southern rim, would Spanish-derived Catholicism be revived in the United States.

French Catholicism in North America

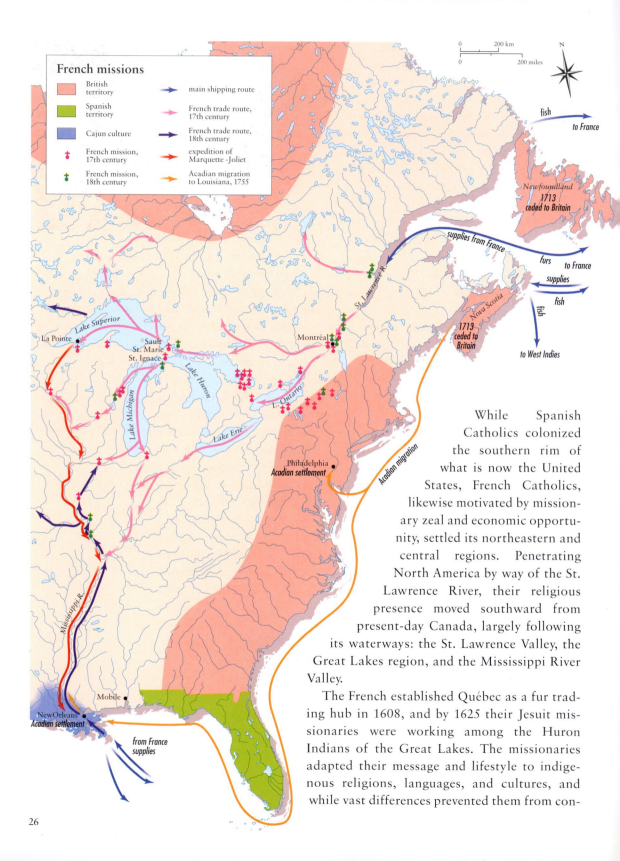

French missions

- British territory
- Spanish territory
- Cajun culture
- French mission, 17th century
- French mission, 18th century
- main shipping route
- French trade route, 17th century
- French trade route, 18th century
- expedition of Marquette -Joliet
- Acadian migration to Louisiana, 1755

Newfoundland
1713 ceded to Britain

fish
to France

supplies from France

furs
to France

supplies

fish

Nova Scotia
1713 ceded to Britain

fish

to West Indies

St. Lawrence R.

Montréal

Lake Superior

La Pointe

Sault St. Marie
St. Ignace

Lake Huron

Lake Michigan

Lake Erie

L. Ontario

Philadelphia
Acadian settlement

Acadian migration

Mississippi R.

Mobile

New Orleans
Acadian settlement

from France
supplies

While Spanish Catholics colonized the southern rim of what is now the United States, French Catholics, likewise motivated by missionary zeal and economic opportunity, settled its northeastern and central regions. Penetrating North America by way of the St. Lawrence River, their religious presence moved southward from present-day Canada, largely following its waterways: the St. Lawrence Valley, the Great Lakes region, and the Mississippi River Valley.

The French established Québec as a fur trading hub in 1608, and by 1625 their Jesuit missionaries were working among the Huron Indians of the Great Lakes. The missionaries adapted their message and lifestyle to indigenous religions, languages, and cultures, and while vast differences prevented them from converting more than a handful of Indians, their mild approach and the economic and military benefits they offered combined to keep the Hurons open to their activities. Iroquois attacks beginning in 1648 disrupted Jesuit activity among the Hurons, but the missionaries retained their ties to the Hurons while also establishing ties with the Iroquois. By 1668 they had established several missions to the Iroquois in upstate New York. After 1680 they began work

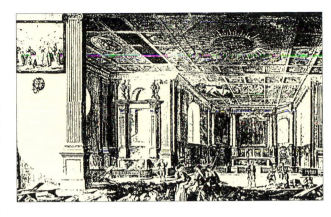

Jesuit College and Church in Québec, as depicted in 1759 by Richard Shortt. Jesuits established a lasting French Catholic culture in the region.

among the Abenaki of what is now Maine. These efforts were continually challenged by rival Dutch and British traders and did not survive the large-scale English movement into the area that began in the late 17th century.

French Jesuits had begun working among the Ottawa of the Illinois country by the 1630s and in subsequent decades founded several missions around the Great Lakes, including La Pointe in northern Wisconsin (1665), and Sault St. Marie (1668) and St. Ignace (1670) in northern Michigan. Jesuit activity expanded southward into the Mississippi Valley after Father Jacques Marquette (1637–75) set out from La Pointe with Louis Joliet (1645–1700) in 1673 to journey down the Mississippi River. Missionaries and fur trappers followed, and by 1682 the French government had claimed all the territory drained by the river and its tributaries and called it Louisiana. By the early 1700s, Jesuits were missionizing among the Natchez of the lower Mississippi, had formed a parish in what became Mobile, Alabama, and made New Orleans a major colonial center from which they evangelized the Choctaw, Alibamon, Arkansas, and other peoples of the region.

Just north of New Orleans, an enduring pocket of French Catholic culture began to develop later in the 17th century with the arrival of French Catholics from Acadia (Nova Scotia). Settled by the French in the early 17th century and ceded to Great Britain in 1713, Acadia remained home to several thousand French Catholics until their expulsion by Britain in 1755. They dispersed through the British colonies to the south, and a large group eventually settled in French-speaking southern Louisiana. Their Acadian culture and Catholicism thereafter developed, through periods of Spanish and then American rule, into the forms we call "Cajun."

The vestiges of colonial French Catholicism in the United States remain most pronounced—though generally weak—in Louisiana. Outside that region, French Catholicism exerted influence not through descendants of French colonizers but by French clergy who emigrated after the French Revolution and assumed important positions in an emerging American Catholic church hierarchy.

Russian Orthodoxy Colonizes America

Not all European colonization of North America was transatlantic and westward-moving. Beginning in the late 18th century, Russian Orthodox missionaries and entrepreneurs approached from northeast Asia, moving eastward across the Bering Sea and north Pacific to trap furs and convert natives in North America.

Russian exploration of North America began with the 1728

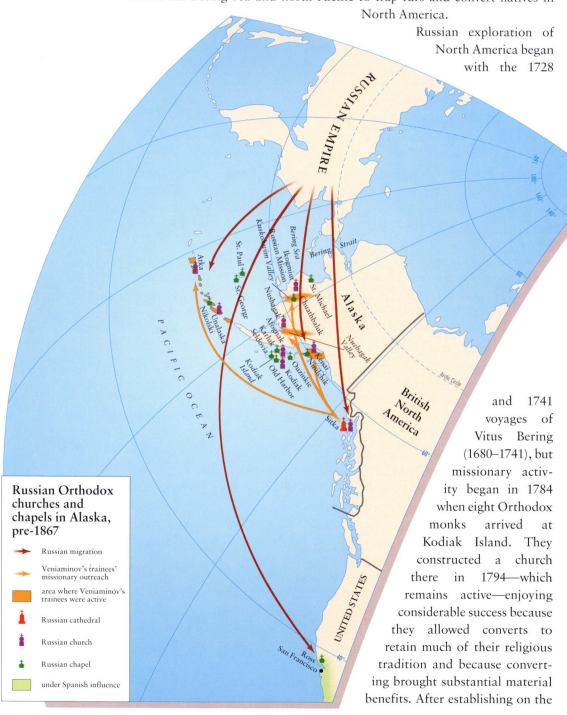

Russian Orthodox churches and chapels in Alaska, pre-1867

➤ Russian migration

➤ Veniaminov's trainees' missionary outreach

▮ area where Veniaminov's trainees were active

⬧ Russian cathedral

⬧ Russian church

⬧ Russian chapel

▮ under Spanish influence

and 1741 voyages of Vitus Bering (1680–1741), but missionary activity began in 1784 when eight Orthodox monks arrived at Kodiak Island. They constructed a church there in 1794—which remains active—enjoying considerable success because they allowed converts to retain much of their religious tradition and because converting brought substantial material benefits. After establishing on the southern Alaskan coast a string of settlements named for Eastern Orthodox saints—Three Saints Harbor (1784), Fort St. George (1787), St. Paul's Harbor (1791), St. Nicholas (1791), and St. Constantin (1793)—they expanded their missionary reach to the Aleutian Islands and the Alaskan interior.

In 1799, Czar Paul I founded the Russian-American Company, required as a government agency to promote the established Orthodox church. But its relations with indigenous Alaskans was tense, for it virtually enslaved male Aleuts and other natives to work in fur trapping, pressured (later, legally required) them to convert, and founded New Archangel (Sitka)—which became an administrative center for both company and Church—on the site of an ancient Tlingit village. Sitka faced hostility from many local natives but eventually developed a multiethnic Russian-Indian population. Company relations with natives, and missionary success, improved after 1821, when the company revised its charter to ameliorate working conditions and step up its support for Orthodox evangelism.

Russian Orthodox activity in Alaska accelerated with the 1834 arrival in Sitka of Ivan Veniaminov (1797–1879), who became Bishop Innocent when Sitka became an official diocese in 1840. The first Orthodox bishop to serve in the Americas, he contributed significantly to the long-term survival of Orthodoxy in the region. During his tenure, the number of churches, chapels, and converts rose substantially—particularly at sites occupied by the company—and the first Orthodox cathedral in the Americas was constructed at Sitka (1848). He also, in 1841, established a seminary at Sitka which trained a native and creole clergy for missionary work throughout the Aleutians, the Kenai Peninsula, the Kuskokwim and Nushagak valleys, and other parts of Alaska.

Russian settlement spread southward to northern California in search of furs, trade advantages, and an agricultural base for the northern settlements. The company sent expeditions to Spanish San Francisco and environs in 1806 and in 1812, when it established Ross (from the word for "Russia") north of the Bay area. But the colony foundered: it never numbered more than a few hundred, never secured official Church recognition of the settlement or consecration of its chapel, never held regular worship services, and was hampered in its agricultural production by coastal fogs. Spanish control, meanwhile, limited expansion into the fertile interior valleys. In 1841, the company sold Ross and its chapel to Sacramento entrepreneur John Sutter.

By 1867, American and British competition in the region had led Russia to sell Alaska to the United States and concentrate more fully on its Asian territories. The Church retained its American property, continued missionizing, and appealed to natives as a buffer against Americanization. It eventually (1905) moved its official American seat to New York to reach out to new Orthodox arrivals from eastern Europe. But Native Americans remained its largest constituency, their creolized religions and cultures permanent legacies of a once Russianized America.

PART III: COLONIAL FORMATIONS, 1607–1800

The settlement of North America by Protestant England was in significant part an act of religiously inspired nationalism designed to counteract the colonial presence of Roman Catholic Spain and France. English visions of a Protestant America were aided by the geography of the Atlantic coast, whose wide and navigable rivers, fertile river valleys, large bays, and fine harbors were conducive to settlement, agriculture, and commerce and allowed the English rapidly to establish a string of prosperous seaboard colonies. By the mid-18th century, the English controlled North America from the Atlantic coast to the Appalachian mountains. The subsequent westward spread of Anglo-American culture after the American Revolution, coupled with the decline of French and Spanish power in North America, meant that English Protestantism, transformed by American experience, would have a profound defining influence on religious and cultural life in the United States.

Perhaps one should say "Protestantisms," for the colonists brought with them the many varieties of English Protestantism that had developed during the 16th and 17th centuries. England colonized North America amid intense religious division and political turmoil. It had been an officially Protestant nation since Henry VIII's 1534 rupture with the Roman Catholic Church and founding of the government-supported ("*established*") Church of England (or *Anglican* church), but many felt that the new church remained corrupted by Roman doctrines and practices and proposed competing visions of England's

The establishment of Jamestown by English Protestants in 1607 was depicted on this map by John White. Protestantism became the dominant religion in America.

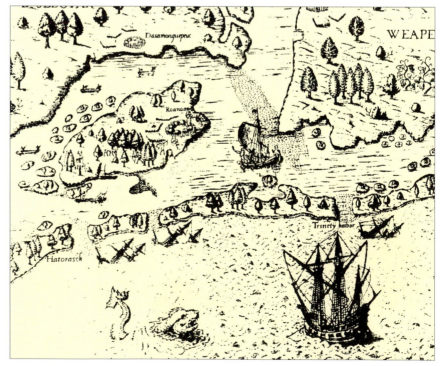

religious future. Aiming to purify the Church of England were *Puritans*, who favored an austere Calvinist theology of total divine sovereignty and human depravity, stricter standards of personal behavior and church membership, an end to bishops' authority, and THE elimination of "Romish" liturgies. Others, called "Separatists," repudiated the Anglican church altogether. Puritans differed among themselves on whether church membership should be confined to confirmed believers; whether church governance should rest with elected representatives (the *Presbyterian* position) or the autonomous congregation (the *Congregationalist* position); whether clerical mediators between God and the individual were unnecessary (the position of *Quakers* and others); and whether only adult believers should be baptized (the *Baptist* position). Differing positions on these issues became the bases for the variety of groups that proliferated in England, particularly during the 1650s, when the national church establishment was for a time displaced by the Puritans' temporary seizure of the government.

Emigrating to the colonies for various religious, economic, and political reasons, members of these groups coexisted uneasily in a new geographic setting that powerfully shaped their development—both individually and in relation to each other—and prevented a duplication of the British religious landscape. Oceanic separation from England and the challenges posed by frontier conditions were particularly important factors, weakening the state-supported Anglican church but allowing dissenting groups to survive—even flourish— and, in some cases, to achieve political power and regional dominance. Relative tolerance in Rhode Island and the mid-Atlantic colonies, meanwhile, fostered diverse groups of dissenters. The weakness of the English religious establishment, the scattered and fragmented nature of seaboard settlement, distance from Europe, and, in some colonies, official toleration also attracted many non-English and/or non-Protestant groups, including Lutherans, Reformed, Mennonites, Moravians, Dunkers, Catholics, Jews, and others.

The result was considerable religious diversity, mostly but not entirely Protestant. The pluralism of the colonial environment undermined the European tradition of established churches and helped generate the open model that became encoded in the First Amendment of the United States Constitution. Still, English Protestant dominion and a powerful shared sense of English Protestant identity among most colonists were central facts of colonial religious life. French Catholics to the north Indian groups to the west loomed to many English colonists as obstacles to a divine plan of Anglo-Protestant expansion, and violence either religiously motivated or religiously sanctioned ensued. A Great Awakening further enhanced the cohesiveness of an emerging Anglo-Protestant culture by infusing it with an ecumenical evangelicalism that would become central to American religious life. By the time of the American Revolution, interpreted by many ministers in terms of Protestant destiny, the landscape east of the Appalachian mountains had already become substantially Protestantized.

The Church of England in Colonial America

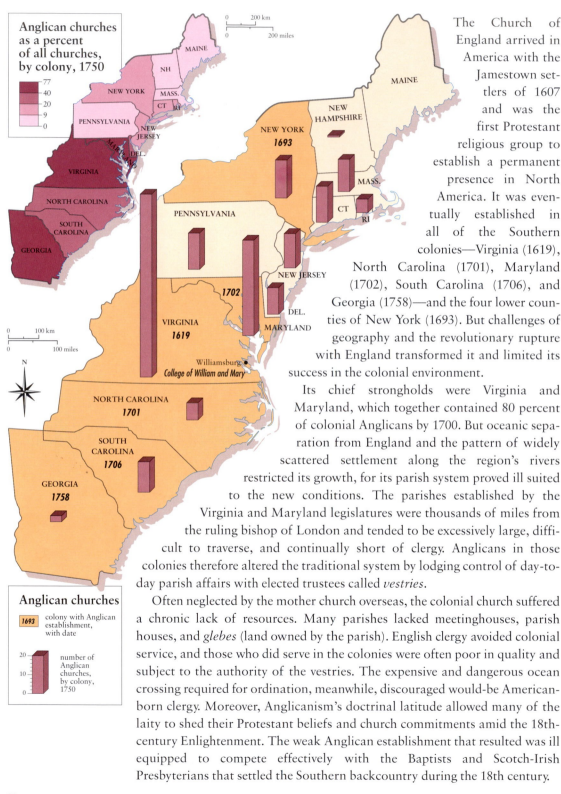

Anglican churches as a percent of all churches, by colony, 1750

- 77
- 40
- 20
- 9
- 0

Anglican churches

1693 — colony with Anglican establishment, with date

20 / 10 / 0 — number of Anglican churches, by colony, 1750

The Church of England arrived in America with the Jamestown settlers of 1607 and was the first Protestant religious group to establish a permanent presence in North America. It was eventually established in all of the Southern colonies—Virginia (1619), North Carolina (1701), Maryland (1702), South Carolina (1706), and Georgia (1758)—and the four lower counties of New York (1693). But challenges of geography and the revolutionary rupture with England transformed it and limited its success in the colonial environment.

Its chief strongholds were Virginia and Maryland, which together contained 80 percent of colonial Anglicans by 1700. But oceanic separation from England and the pattern of widely scattered settlement along the region's rivers restricted its growth, for its parish system proved ill suited to the new conditions. The parishes established by the Virginia and Maryland legislatures were thousands of miles from the ruling bishop of London and tended to be excessively large, difficult to traverse, and continually short of clergy. Anglicans in those colonies therefore altered the traditional system by lodging control of day-to-day parish affairs with elected trustees called *vestries*.

Often neglected by the mother church overseas, the colonial church suffered a chronic lack of resources. Many parishes lacked meetinghouses, parish houses, and *glebes* (land owned by the parish). English clergy avoided colonial service, and those who did serve in the colonies were often poor in quality and subject to the authority of the vestries. The expensive and dangerous ocean crossing required for ordination, meanwhile, discouraged would-be American-born clergy. Moreover, Anglicanism's doctrinal latitude allowed many of the laity to shed their Protestant beliefs and church commitments amid the 18th-century Enlightenment. The weak Anglican establishment that resulted was ill equipped to compete effectively with the Baptists and Scotch-Irish Presbyterians that settled the Southern backcountry during the 18th century.

To be sure, Anglicanism was the second-largest colonial denomination in 1700, encompassing more than a hundred churches from Massachusetts to South Carolina. After the 1701 founding in Maryland of the Society for the Propagation of the Gospel in Foreign Parts (SPG), which provided a crucial transoceanic link to England, it enjoyed even greater strength and institutional presence. The SPG financed the construction of church buildings and sponsored more than 300 colonial missionaries—especially in Puritan New England—by the end of the American Revolution. It was less successful among Indians and slaves than among whites, but key conversions among Pennsylvania Quakers and Connecticut Congregationalists generated substantial growth in those colonies.

Still, the church remained weak, and events of the 18th century weakened it further. Southerners fired by the Great Awakening's antiestablishment message—especially those in the backcountry—were inclined to mistrust Anglican tepidity toward revivalism and its perceived association with the tidewater gentry. Anglicans themselves divided into prorevival and antirevival parties beginning in the 1760s. The onset of the American Revolution increased suspicions of Anglicanism nationwide, for Anglican clergy were suspected of loyalism, and the SPG's push for an American bishop in the 1760s added a religious dimension to American fears of British imperial power. The migration of Anglican clergy who were in fact loyalist aggravated the church's institutional anemia, as did its disestablishment in America in the 1780s at the hands of dissenting Rationalists, Baptists, and Presbyterians.

The Church of England survived in the geographic and political isolation of the new United States, but only after an agreement by English bishops to consecrate American bishops paved the way for ordinations west of the Atlantic, and only after it changed its name to the Protestant Episcopal Church in the United States of America.

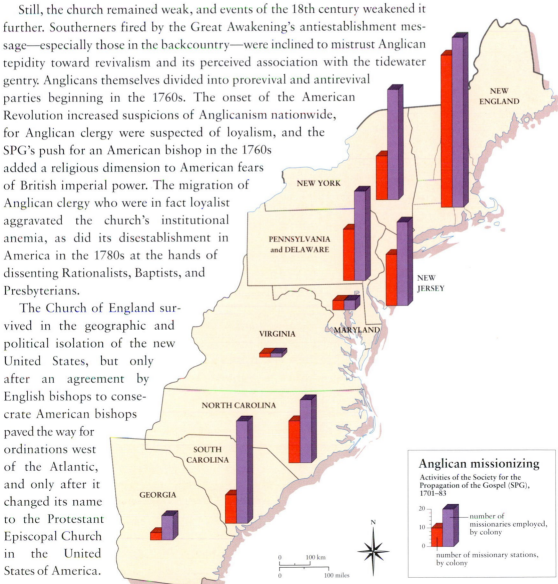

Anglican missionizing

Activities of the Society for the Propagation of the Gospel (SPG), 1701–83

number of missionaries employed, by colony

number of missionary stations, by colony

0   100 km

0   100 miles

N

Puritanism in New England

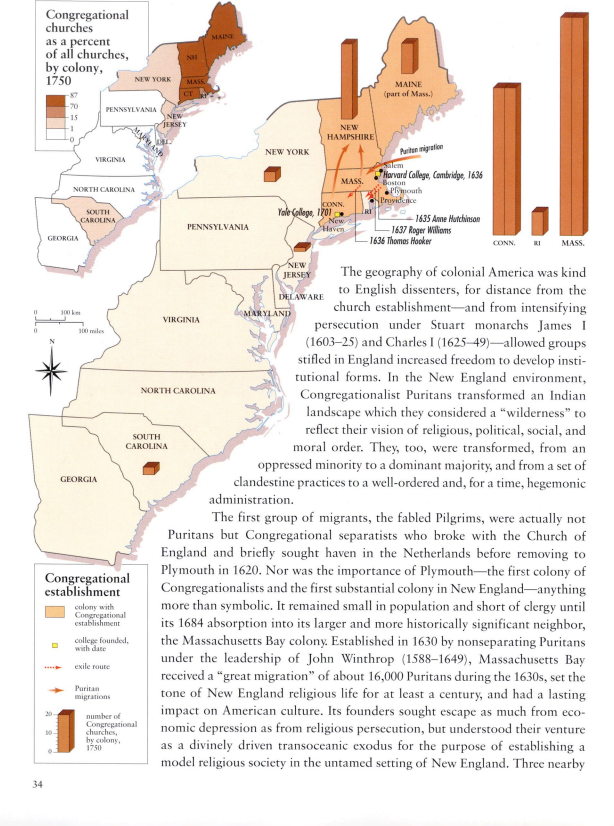

Congregational churches as a percent of all churches, by colony, 1750

- 87
- 70
- 15
- 1
- 0

Puritan migration

Salem
Harvard College, Cambridge, 1636
Boston
Plymouth
Providence

Yale College, 1701
New Haven

1635 Anne Hutchinson
1637 Roger Williams
1636 Thomas Hooker

CONN. RI MASS.

Congregational establishment

- colony with Congregational establishment
- college founded, with date
- ····▶ exile route
- ➤ Puritan migrations
- number of Congregational churches, by colony, 1750 (20 / 10 / 0)

The geography of colonial America was kind to English dissenters, for distance from the church establishment—and from intensifying persecution under Stuart monarchs James I (1603–25) and Charles I (1625–49)—allowed groups stifled in England increased freedom to develop institutional forms. In the New England environment, Congregationalist Puritans transformed an Indian landscape which they considered a "wilderness" to reflect their vision of religious, political, social, and moral order. They, too, were transformed, from an oppressed minority to a dominant majority, and from a set of clandestine practices to a well-ordered and, for a time, hegemonic administration.

The first group of migrants, the fabled Pilgrims, were actually not Puritans but Congregational separatists who broke with the Church of England and briefly sought haven in the Netherlands before removing to Plymouth in 1620. Nor was the importance of Plymouth—the first colony of Congregationalists and the first substantial colony in New England—anything more than symbolic. It remained small in population and short of clergy until its 1684 absorption into its larger and more historically significant neighbor, the Massachusetts Bay colony. Established in 1630 by nonseparating Puritans under the leadership of John Winthrop (1588–1649), Massachusetts Bay received a "great migration" of about 16,000 Puritans during the 1630s, set the tone of New England religious life for at least a century, and had a lasting impact on American culture. Its founders sought escape as much from economic depression as from religious persecution, but understood their venture as a divinely driven transoceanic exodus for the purpose of establishing a model religious society in the untamed setting of New England. Three nearby settlements—Connecticut (1636), New Haven (1638), and Saybrook (1643), which merged in 1662—varied in organizational detail but were similarly conceived, and the migration of Massachusetts and Connecticut families to New Hampshire, first founded in 1630, gave that colony a Puritan stamp as well.

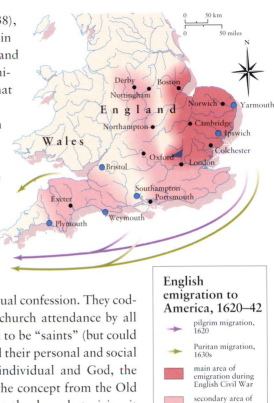

English emigration to America, 1620–42

→ pilgrim migration, 1620
→ Puritan migration, 1630s
▪ main area of emigration during English Civil War
▪ secondary area of emigration during English Civil War
● main port of embarkation

The Puritans based church, state, and society in New England on their reading of biblical precept. Their church ideals, codified in the 1648 Cambridge Platform, included a congregational polity and the restriction of church membership and suffrage to the "saints"—those elected by God to salvation—who alone could be entrusted with the colony's affairs. In a departure from English Puritan practice, they sought to ensure purity of church membership by requiring that applicants receive congregational approval of a publicly presented spiritual confession. They codified biblical law in state law—including required church attendance by all inhabitants—and charged civil magistrates, who had to be "saints" (but could not be ministers), with enforcing it. They understood their personal and social commitments as holy "covenants"—between the individual and God, the group and God, and among themselves—deriving the concept from the Old Testament, medieval contract theory, and Calvinist theology, but giving it added emphasis as they sought to order their new environment.

They Puritanized and, in their fashion, sacralized the "wilderness" in several ways. They intermittently evangelized the local Indians, and John Eliot (1604–90) worked among the Massachuset to create fourteen villages of Anglicized "praying Indians." But within a half-century of settlement they had largely decimated and subdued the native population through English-borne disease and such violent confrontations as the Pequot War (1637) and King Philip's War (1675–76), the last of which destroyed most of the Christianized villages. They interpreted all of these developments as a providential clearing of New England for their mission. Replicating the English landscape and giving visible expression to their sense of collective mission, they built compact and homogeneous villages with meetinghouses at their centers. The meetinghouse itself was a plain structure resembling other buildings, since the Puritans believed that God could not be confined in ordinary space and was therefore not specially present in any one place. Dominated by the pulpit, it was shorn of any adornment that might distract attention from the plain and theologically sophisticated sermon that was at the heart of worship. After the meetinghouse, perhaps the most important mark on the Puritanized landscape was Harvard College, established in 1636 in order to ensure the perpetuation of the educated ministry that New England Puritans deemed essential to the success of their mission.

The seal of the Massachusetts Bay colony conveys the Puritans' sense of religious mission and cultural supremacy.

Their effort was remarkably successful. By 1640, there were already more than twice as many Congregational churches in Massachusetts Bay as there were Anglican churches in Virginia, and, by 1700, Congregationalists had the greatest number of churches in the English colonies: 120 in New England alone, 77 in Massachusetts, 35 in Connecticut, 6 in New Hampshire, and 2 in the portion of Massachusetts that later became the state of Maine. They were weak south of New England—there were only scattered churches in Long Island, Dutch New York, Virginia, South Carolina, and Georgia—but they dominated the northern third of English North America well into the 18th century.

Of course, their hegemony there was neither unchallenged, universal, nor permanent. As early as the 1630s, two vocal dissenters—Anne Hutchinson and Roger Williams—were banished for religious views deemed threatening by the Puritan establishment. Williams established the colony of Rhode Island in 1636, settling at a place he called Providence. This small colony, sandwiched between Massachusetts Bay and Connecticut, was the only one in New England without a Congregational establishment and became a magnet for dissenters from the "New England Way." Later in the century, persecuted English Quakers who had sought refuge there made forays into the surrounding colonies, where their alternative religious message earned them severe punishment at the hands of the establishment.

There were also problems among the Puritans themselves. More favorable English circumstances ended the great migration in the 1640s, leaving zealous Puritans an increasingly small minority among a diversity of religious groups, a growing number of commercially minded settlers, and a new generation of Puritans born in New England and far less prone than their immigrant parents to intense religious experience. This second generation forced a relaxation of church membership standards by 1662. Conservative Puritans began soon thereafter to express fears of decline that had at least some basis in reality. A decisive blow to the Puritan establishment was the English government's recharter of Massachusetts Bay in 1691, requiring religious toleration, ending the religious requirement for suffrage, and installing an Anglican governor and administration. The Salem witch trials of the following year testified to Puritan anxieties over the rapid changes of the late 17th century. In the 18th century, Puritan orthodoxy was threatened by growing theological liberalism; a liberal takeover of the Harvard administration sparked the founding of Yale College by conservative Congregationalists in 1701. The Great Awakening of the 1740s further undermined Puritan influence. A new brand of piety—promoted among others by Yale-educated Congregationalist minister Jonathan Edwards—encouraged enthusiastic preaching and emotional conversion over the plain sermon and theological precision and encouraged criticism of the establishment. Congregationalists became bitterly divided between opponents and supporters of the revival, the latter often bolting to the evangelistic Baptist denomination.

Congregationalism remained vital. The conspicuous involvement of many of its ministers in the agitation of the American Revolution enhanced its reputation in the new nation, and Congregational establishments survived well into the 19th century in Connecticut (1818), New Hampshire (1819), and Massachusetts (1833). Likewise, the Puritan ideology left lasting legacies in American culture in its commitment to education and literacy and its rhetoric of national mission. But by the close of the 18th century, Puritan religion had been highly attenuated and Congregationalism reduced to only one of several denominations amid New England's burgeoning Protestant pluralism.

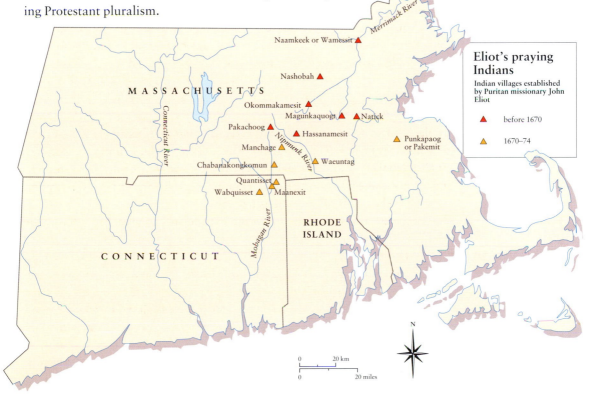

Eliot's praying Indians

Indian villages established by Puritan missionary John Eliot

▲ before 1670

▲ 1670–74

Colonial Presbyterianism

Presbyterianism is a hierarchically and geographically arranged denomination in which congregational representatives in a given locale form governing *presbyteries*. These combine into broader regional *synods* and, at the national level, a General Assembly. Presbyterianism was organized by Scottish Calvinists in the 16th century, many of whom, facing royal disfavor, later migrated to Ireland and then, as "Scotch-Irish," to the English colonies. There, Presbyterianism grew from small beginnings in the 17th century to become large and powerful—if volatile—by the time of the Revolution.

Presbyterians worshiped by 1611 in Jamestown and by the 1630s in Massachusetts and Connecticut, where they associated comfortably with the doctrinally identical Congregationalists. But they concentrated early in the middle colonies. In Long Island and New Jersey, Puritan migrants from New England founded several churches between 1640 and 1700. In Maryland, Scotch-Irish missionary Francis Makemie (1658–1708), who arrived in 1683,

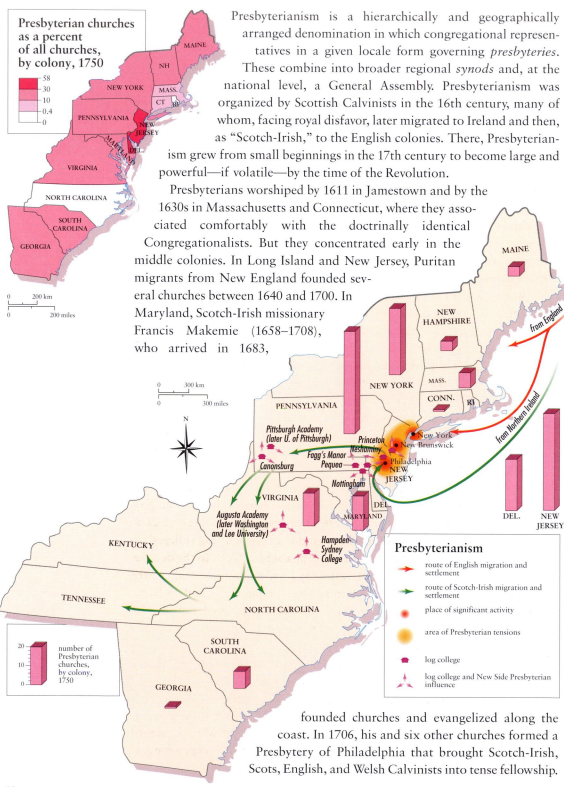

Presbyterian churches as a percent of all churches, by colony, 1750

58
30
10
0.4
0

0   200 km

0   200 miles

Presbyterianism

route of English migration and settlement

route of Scotch-Irish migration and settlement

place of significant activity

area of Presbyterian tensions

log college

log college and New Side Presbyterian influence

number of Presbyterian churches, by colony, 1750

founded churches and evangelized along the coast. In 1706, his and six other churches formed a Presbytery of Philadelphia that brought Scotch-Irish, Scots, English, and Welsh Calvinists into tense fellowship.

This and presbyteries founded over the following decade at Newcastle, Delaware, and on Long Island formed the Synod of Philadelphia in 1717.

The denomination's geographic, ethnic, and doctrinal balance shifted during the half century after 1714, when the policies of England's new Hanover monarchy drove about 200,000 Scotch-Irish and about 50,000 Scottish Presbyterians to the colonies. Most arrived in Philadelphia, moving into western Pennsylvania and then southward through the Shenandoah Valley into western Virginia and the Carolinas. Conflict ensued between the Scotch-Irish and Scottish of the middle colonies, who emphasized doctrinal correctness, and the English of New York and New England, who emphasized personal experience over doctrinal formulas. The Great Awakening of the 1730s and 1740s intensified this conflict. Now Scotch-Irish immigrant William Tennent Sr. (1673?–1746) and his sons embraced revivalism, preached across the Delaware Valley, formed a prorevival Scotch-Irish group that aligned with the English party, attracted followers to their "New Side" Presbyterianism throughout the middle colonies, founded a "Log College" in Neshaminy, Pennsylvania, to train revival preachers, and gathered sympathetic congregations into a New Brunswick (New Jersey) presbytery. In 1741, the antirevival ("Old Side") Synod of Philadelphia ejected New Brunswick, which joined with like-minded presbyteries to form the Synod of New York in 1745.

New Side Presbyterianism flourished, attracting more and more ministers and spreading into western Pennsylvania and the Southern backcountry. It provided the major impulse behind the 1746 founding of the College of New Jersey (later Princeton University), whose graduates opened "log colleges" in Pennsylvania, Virginia, and, later, the trans-Appalachian West. In the decades that followed, New Side itinerant revivalists sparked denominational growth among the Scotch-Irish and others settling the Virginia and Carolina backcountry. In 1758—by which time the New Side dominated outside the Philadelphia area's Old Side Scotch-Irish enclave—Old Side leaders rejoined them in the Synod of New York and Philadelphia.

By the eve of the American Revolution, Presbyterians were outnumbered only by Congregationalists. They were a particularly strong force in the backcountry South, figuring prominently in the 1780s drive to disestablish Anglicanism. Having used revivalism to reach an expanding frontier population, the Presbyterian Church in the United States of America, which convened its first General Assembly in 1788, was well prepared for the competitive and pluralistic religious environment of the new nation.

The Rise and Fall of Quaker Regions

Colonial geography was a mixed blessing for the Society of Friends, or Quakers. Distance from England allowed them to establish not only institutional forms but, in some places, regional prominence and even political dominance. But the local geography also offered commercial opportunities that challenged their ideals.

Formed by George Fox (1624–91) in England in the 1650s, the Quakers spread their radical message of intense personal communion with a divine "inner light" from their early base in northern England first to London and southern England and then, by the late 1650s, to the West Indies and North American colonies. They organized into geographically defined and increasingly encompassing monthly, quarterly, and yearly meetings which sought through participants' "inner light" to forge consensus. But established authorities perceived their questioning of outward institutions, worldly power structures, and social distinctions (including those based on race and gender) as threatening.

Engraving of a Quaker meeting. Quakers were persecuted in England and New England but enjoyed political dominance in colonial Pennsylvania.

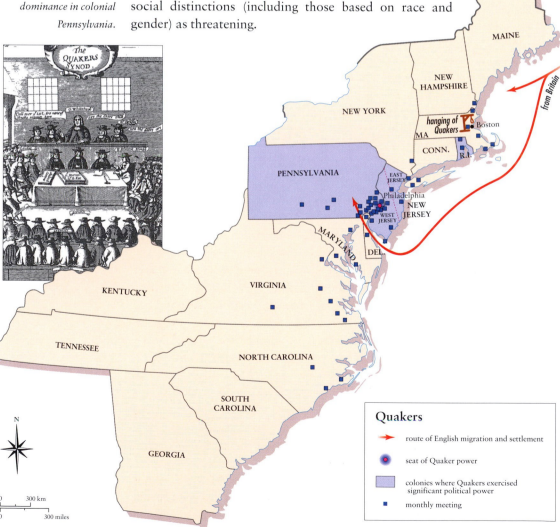

Quakers

→ route of English migration and settlement

● seat of Quaker power

▢ colonies where Quakers exercised significant political power

■ monthly meeting

0   300 km
0   300 miles

Seeking haven and converts, Quakers arrived in New England beginning in 1656 and met with a hostile response. Massachusetts Bay, Plymouth, Connecticut, and New Haven outlawed Quakerism almost immediately, and severe enforcement—in some instances through execution—forced Quakers to settle at first in such remote areas as Cape Cod, Nantucket, and Maine. In tolerant Rhode Island, they attained majority status and control of the General Assembly. Yet they established their presence throughout the region during the 1660s and convened their first New England Yearly Meeting in 1661. The weakness of the Anglican establishment in Virginia and Maryland allowed Quakers to develop numerous local meetings during the 1660s and yearly meetings by 1673. In North Carolina, where Anglicanism was particularly slow to develop, Quakers organized effectively—a North Carolina meeting was formed in 1681—and remained the colony's only organized denomination until 1701. Yet their prominence there waned after Anglicans assumed control in the early 18th century and antislavery principles led them to migrate from the Southern states to the Midwest in the early 19th.

The most significant Quaker presence was in the Delaware Valley. Quaker merchants purchased East and West Jersey in the 1670s, controlling both until New Jersey became a royal colony in 1702. On the west bank of the river, William Penn (1644–1718) founded Pennsylvania in 1681 as an experiment in applied Quakerism. Its assembly, controlled by Quakers until 1756, reached consensual decisions, enacted religious freedom, eliminated oaths, refused to establish a militia, outlawed slavery in 1711, and extended special protection to Indians and the poor. Friends in the region formed the Philadelphia Yearly Meeting in 1685, and numbered about 50,000 by 1750. Meanwhile, Philadelphia, near the mouth of the Delaware, became a bustling seaport.

The Quakers were, however, too close to both London and Philadelphia. Their power was shaken after the Glorious Revolution of 1688 ended Penn's royal favor, Anglicans began to challenge their dominance, and they became divided among themselves into rival urban-cosmopolitan and rural-conservative factions. Over the first half of the 18th century, waning numerical dominance and the ever-growing strains of political supremacy and commercial prosperity gradually undermined their ability to keep their government grounded in Quaker principles. They finally renounced political power in 1756 amid the intense geopolitical rivalries of the French and Indian War.

Discernible Quaker regions ceased to exist by the early 19th century, but their contributions to the later antislavery and women's rights movements testified to their continuing impact on American life.

Quaker migration from the British Isles

→ spread of Quakerism

→ main migration route

Scotland

Edinburgh

Ireland · Dublin

England

Wales

London

to New England and Pennsylvania

0 — 100 km
0 — 100 miles

N

The Rise of the Baptists

The Baptists experienced a meteoric rise after 1740, propelled by revivalism, revolution, and geographic expansion from a tiny and obscure sect to the forefront of American religious life.

As radical products of the Protestant Reformation, Baptists, like English Puritans, embraced congregational autonomy, exclusive church membership, and (usually) Calvinist theology. But they differed from Puritans in restricting baptism to consenting believers and in opposing state religious regulations. They were themselves divided—"Particular" (or "Regular") Baptists, holding to Calvinist predestination, and "General" Baptists, embracing free will, formed separate regional associations—but their common convictions unified them against English and colonial religious establishments.

Calvinist Baptists arrived in New England with the Puritan migration but were unwelcome there from the start. They gravitated to Rhode Island, where founder Roger Williams embraced their position for a time after his banishment from Massachusetts and established a Baptist church at Providence (1639). Baptists opened a second church in Newport shortly thereafter. But internal theological differences and Puritan strength in the rest of the region stifled their growth, and by 1660 there were only four Baptist churches in Rhode Island. Growth was similarly sluggish elsewhere in New England. A Baptist church founded in Boston (1665) was joined by only scattered others in Massachusetts, while in Connecticut no Baptist church appeared until 1706, and a second not until two decades later.

In the middle colonies, toleration and the absence of religious establishments attracted Baptists from Rhode Island, Ireland, and Wales beginning in the 1680s, especially to the Philadelphia area. By the 18th century, the region became a focus of Baptist strength. The Philadelphia Baptist Association, formed in 1707 by five Particular Delaware Valley congregations, expanded to include churches in Maryland, Virginia, New York, and Connecticut, with ties to Baptists in Massachusetts and the Carolinas, and became an intercolonial center for Regular Baptists. It provided doctrinal unity, ordained ministers, helped found new churches and regional associations, and sent out missionaries to whites and Indians. It also arranged the 1764 founding of the College of Rhode Island (later Brown University), which trained and recruited clergy and became a denominational intellectual hub. But the denomination remained small and diffuse throughout the colonies until well into the 18th century.

The Great Awakening was a turning point, for its antiauthoritarian message and call for regenerate churches meshed well with Baptist belief and practice. Baptists made dramatic gains in rural and backcountry New England, where more than a hundred revival-fired Congregational churches bolted the estab-

Separate Congregationalist bodies becoming Baptist, 1740s–1750s

● new Baptist body

MAINE

NEW HAMPSHIRE

NEW YORK

MASSACHUSETTS

CONN.

RI

NEW JERSEY

N

0   100 km

0   100 miles

lishment to become "Separate Congregationalists" and then, in many cases, Baptists. These new Baptist congregations formed the Warren (Rhode Island) Baptist Association in 1767. Shubal Stearns (1706–71) and other newly converted Baptists went from New England to the Southern backcountry, where, aided by the Philadelphia Association and rising anti-Anglican sentiment, they founded several new Baptist congregations and, in 1758, the Sandy Creek (North Carolina) Association.

There were nearly 500 Baptist churches by the time of the American Revolution, and growth accelerated thereafter because Baptist advocacy of church-state separation and disestablishment became intertwined with the revolutionary cause. Emphasizing local autonomy and individual freedom, and accustomed to attracting voluntary support by sparking religious enthusiasm, the denomination proved particularly well suited to the democratic ethos and westward expansion of the new nation. Its growth to more than 1,100 churches by 1797 anticipated its imminent rise to national preeminence.

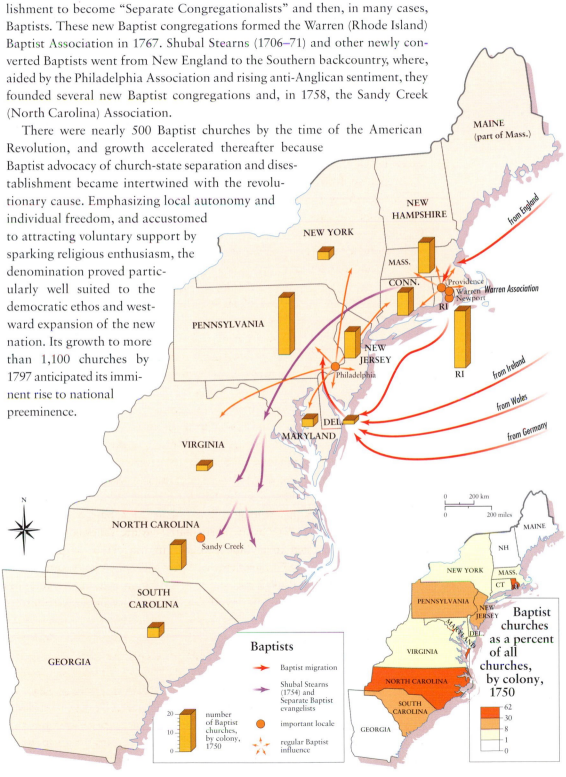

MAINE
(part of Mass.)

NEW HAMPSHIRE

from England

NEW YORK

MASS.

CONN.

Providence
Warren   Warren Association
Newport
RI

PENNSYLVANIA

NEW JERSEY

RI

from Ireland

Philadelphia

from Wales

DEL.
MARYLAND

from Germany

VIRGINIA

N

NORTH CAROLINA

Sandy Creek

SOUTH CAROLINA

GEORGIA

0   200 km
0   200 miles

MAINE

NH

NEW YORK   MASS.
CT
PENNSYLVANIA   RI
NEW
JERSEY
DEL.

VIRGINIA

Baptist
churches
as a percent
of all
churches,
by colony,
1750

NORTH CAROLINA

SOUTH
CAROLINA

GEORGIA

62
30
8
1
0

Baptists

→ Baptist migration

→ Shubal Stearns (1754) and Separate Baptist evangelists

● important locale

✳ regular Baptist influence

20
10
0
number of Baptist churches, by colony, 1750

The Development of American Methodism

Methodism emerged only in the mid-18th century and therefore arrived late on the colonial scene, but its techniques produced growth as rapid and geographically widespread as that of the Baptists.

The denomination began as a renewal movement within Anglicanism led by John Wesley (1703–91), who as an Oxford student joined a prayer and Bible study group called "Methodist" because of its methodical conscientiousness and discipline. He later began open-air preaching and organizing small lay-conducted "societies" and smaller classes for prayer, study, emotional fellowship, mutual discipline, and the cultivation of personal holiness. Lay preachers coordinated the groups, traveling regular circuits and meeting in an annual conference led by Wesley. The movement spread in England and Ireland—worrying the Anglican church—and then, in the 1760s, to the colonies.

Methodism found particularly fertile environments in Maryland and Virginia, where the effects of the Great Awakening were being felt and the Anglican laity, if not clergy, provided a ready audience for revival; in the middle colonies, which lacked resisting establishments; and in urban areas, where population density promoted organization. Maryland especially became an early stronghold. New Yorkers formed a society in 1766 and built Wesley Chapel in 1768, while Philadelphia Methodists formed a class in 1768 and in 1769 purchased a church. After Wesley sent a corps of preachers to the colonies between 1769 and 1773, revivals flared in Virginia. The most notable agent was Francis Asbury (1745–1816), who arrived in 1771, established headquarters in Baltimore, helped erect two churches there, was named "superintendent of the American Colonies" in 1772, and eventually logged some 250,000 miles of circuit riding. By 1773, when colonial Methodist ministers convened their first conference in Philadelphia, they counted 1160 members in Maryland (with nearly half), Philadelphia, New York, New Jersey, and Virginia.

During the American Revolution, the departure of Methodist preachers sharing Wesley's loyalism left Asbury and native patriot evangelists to develop the movement, and the departure of loyalist Anglican clergy left many practicing Methodists without the sacraments. Wesley opposed attempts by unordained American Methodist preachers to administer the sacraments, but eventually approved both their ordination and the formation of an independent American church when confronted by the lack of colonial clergy, popular American suspicion

Old Yellow Meeting House, Inlaystown, New Jersey, built 1766.

of Anglicanism, and independence sentiment. The Methodist Episcopal Church, led by Asbury, was formed in Baltimore in 1784.

Methodism's emphasis on personal growth, self-discipline, and lay leadership attracted many Americans, particularly in new areas of settlement, and its facility of organization and use of circuit riders prepared it for success on the sparsely settled Western frontier. It therefore experienced explosive numerical and geographic growth. In the 1780s, Methodists began evangelizing South Carolina and New England, and pushing westward to western Pennsylvania, western North Carolina, Kentucky, and Tennessee. Circuits existed in all of these places before the decade ended. Itinerant preachers in the isolated settlements of the frontier accentuated Methodism's emphasis on enthusiastic prayer and Bible study and jettisoned Wesley's sacramentalism—but those who swelled Methodist membership from 8,504 in 1780 to nearly 60,000 a decade later (and would soon join in much larger numbers) did not seem to mind.

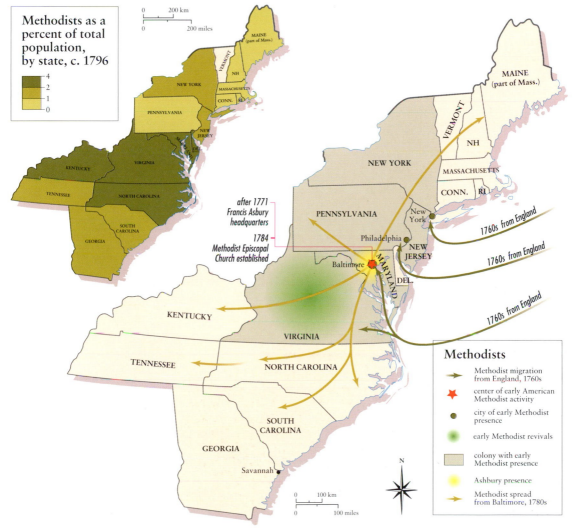

Methodists as a percent of total population, by state, c. 1796

- 4
- 2
- 1
- 0

after 1771
Francis Asbury headquarters

1784
Methodist Episcopal Church established

1760s from England

Methodists

→ Methodist migration from England, 1760s

★ center of early American Methodist activity

● city of early Methodist presence

early Methodist revivals

colony with early Methodist presence

Ashbury presence

→ Methodist spread from Baltimore, 1780s

45

Lutheran and Reformed Groups

Lutheran and Reformed Protestants constituted most of British North America's white non-British population and considerably enriched its ethnic and Protestant pluralism. Both groups trace their origins to the Protestant reformers of the 16th century, both are biblically grounded faiths emphasizing salvation by the grace of a sovereign God, and both spread through northern and western Europe during the 16th and 17th centuries. Rejecting the icons, crosses, and—except for baptism and communion—the sacraments of Roman Catholicism, they insisted that devotion focus on Jesus and the text of the Bible.

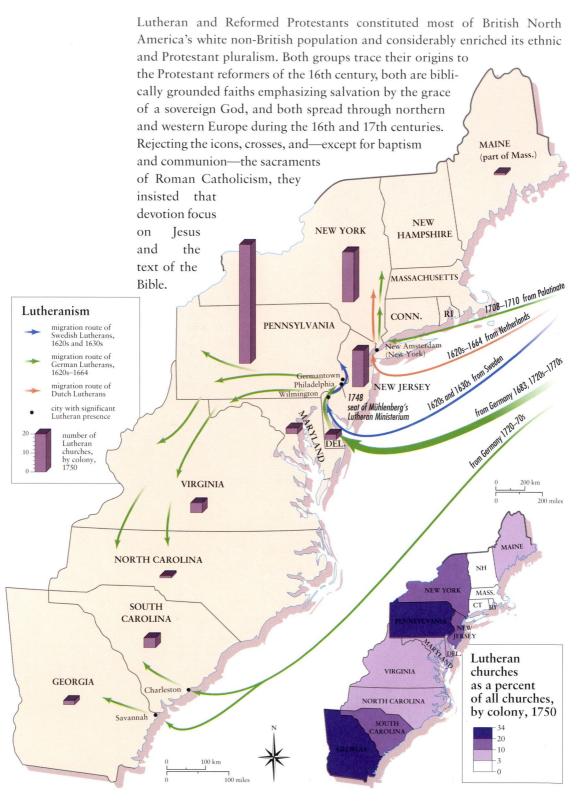

Lutheranism

→ migration route of Swedish Lutherans, 1620s and 1630s

→ migration route of German Lutherans, 1620s–1664

→ migration route of Dutch Lutherans

• city with significant Lutheran presence

number of Lutheran churches, by colony, 1750

MAINE (part of Mass.)

NEW YORK

NEW HAMPSHIRE

MASSACHUSETTS

CONN.   RI

1708–1710 from Palatinate

1620s–1664 from Netherlands

PENNSYLVANIA

New Amsterdam (New York)

1620s and 1630s from Sweden

from Germany 1683, 1720s–1770s

NEW JERSEY

Germantown
Philadelphia
Wilmington

from Germany 1720–70s

1748 seat of Mühlenberg's Lutheran Ministerium

MARYLAND

DEL.

VIRGINIA

NORTH CAROLINA

SOUTH CAROLINA

GEORGIA

Charleston

Savannah

N

0   100 km
0   100 miles

0   200 km
0   200 miles

MAINE
NH
NEW YORK
MASS.
CT   RI
PENNSYLVANIA
NEW JERSEY
DEL.
MARYLAND
VIRGINIA
NORTH CAROLINA
SOUTH CAROLINA
GEORGIA

Lutheran churches as a percent of all churches, by colony, 1750

34
20
10
3
0

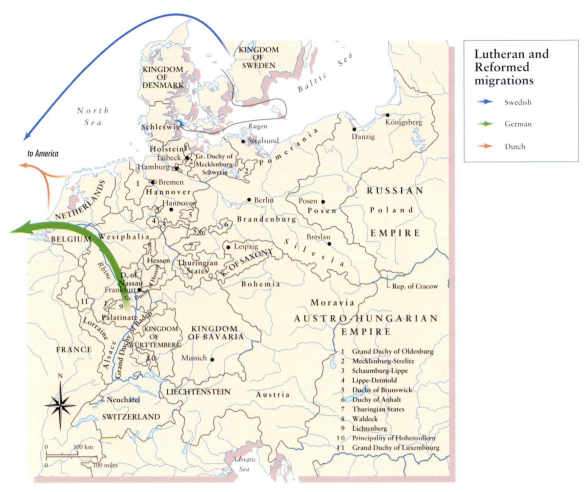

Legend for map:

Lutheran and Reformed migrations

- → Swedish
- → German
- → Dutch

1. Grand Duchy of Oldenburg
2. Mecklenburg-Strelitz
3. Schaumburg-Lippe
4. Lippe-Detmold
5. Duchy of Brunswick
6. Duchy of Anhalt
7. Thuringian States
8. Waldeck
9. Lichtenberg
10. Principality of Hohenzollern
11. Grand Duchy of Luxembourg

America's first Lutherans were Swedish settlers who founded New Sweden in the Delaware River Valley during the 1630s and their first congregation at Wilmington, Delaware, in 1638. The Dutch annexed this colony in 1655, and its 400 inhabitants came under the control of the Dutch Reformed, who had established New Netherland in the nearby lower Hudson River Valley and the city of New Amsterdam on the southern tip of Manhattan Island in 1626. The Dutch Reformed became a strong regional presence, establishing eleven churches in New Netherland before the British seized it in 1664 and more than 70 in English-ruled New York and New Jersey by 1750, as well as Queen's College (later Rutgers University) and a theological seminary in New Brunswick, New Jersey. New Netherland's Lutherans, Swedish and Dutch, were coerced into Reformed worship and adopted elements of that tradition, but under English rule established their own congregations—the first at New York and Albany—and a council joining Lutherans throughout the Hudson and Delaware valleys. Another and much smaller Reformed group, the French Reformed (called Huguenots), remained inchoate and formed only a handful of congregations around Boston, New York, and Charleston that were eventually absorbed by other ethnic Reformed groups.

Germans were by far the most substantial ethnic element of the Lutheran and Reformed presence. Attracted by Penn's policies, they migrated largely from the Palatinate (a Rhine River Valley area in southern Germany) to Pennsylvania in 1683 and founded Germantown near Philadelphia. During the mid-18th century, German Lutherans and Reformed engaged in a large transatlantic migration of about 65,000—which with natural increase elevated their American numbers to more than 225,000 by 1776 and contributed to a diverse back-country religious culture as they joined the Scotch-Irish westward and southward

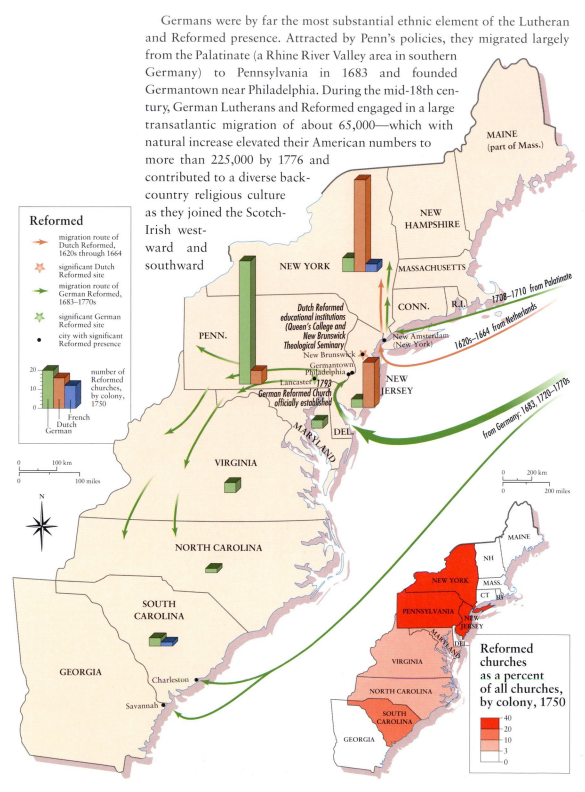

Reformed

→ migration route of Dutch Reformed, 1620s through 1664

★ significant Dutch Reformed site

→ migration route of German Reformed, 1683–1770s

★ significant German Reformed site

• city with significant Reformed presence

number of Reformed churches, by colony, 1750

French
Dutch
German

Reformed churches as a percent of all churches, by colony, 1750

40
20
10
3
0

migration into western Maryland, Virginia, and North Carolina. Despite their spread along the frontier, a substantial German Reformed migration to the Hudson River Valley from 1708 to 1710, a sizable German Lutheran presence in New York and New Jersey, and the erection of several churches by both groups in the Southern seaports, the region north and west of Philadelphia remained for Germans the major focal point of settlement.

Physical and cultural geography—including shared ethnicity and language, Anglophone dominance, isolation from their European church organizations, a shortage of clergy and other resources, competition from various German sects, and the challenges of institution-building on the frontier—moved German Lutherans and Reformed to such cooperative measures as shared buildings and hymnals and to increased reliance on lay pastors. Yet they maintained separate communions and clergy, and eventually formed separate organizations. German Reformed congregations formed a Coetus in 1747 and the German Reformed Church in Lancaster, Pennsylvania, in 1793, while German Lutherans formed a governing Ministerium of Pennsylvania in 1748.

Their continuing use of the German language operated to keep both groups ethnically exclusive, their growth fueled largely by continuing immigration and natural increase. Yet they also contended with an emergent American culture. They were often sympathetic to the new revivalism of the 18th and early 19th centuries—which had some German roots—and German Reformed in particular were readily moved by the patriotism of the American Revolution to jettison their European language and theology. Lutherans were more conflicted, with those in urban and backcountry areas, where they were often in the minority, defending ethnic tradition less tenaciously than their counterparts in all-German rural areas. Amid the pluralism of the cities and the revivals of the trans-Appalachian frontier, they embraced the English services, ecumenical cooperation, and evangelicalism of their Anglo-Protestant neighbors.

Old Lutheran Church in Philadelphia, 1800. Lutherans and other German religious groups were particularly prominent in Southeastern Pennsylvania.

German Sectarians in British America

A significant minority of German migration to colonial America consisted of Mennonites, Amish, Moravians, and Dunkers who accepted William Penn's 1677 invitation to Pennsylvania. Called Anabaptist (meaning "rebaptism"), these radical Protestant sects emerged in 16th-century central Europe, believing the New Testament to require adult baptism, foot washing, pacifism, and withdrawal from the corrupt governments and churches of the "world" into exclusive communities based on simple living and plain dress. These groups were persecuted, but spread through Switzerland, the Netherlands, and Germany's Rhine Valley.

Mennonites, the main early Anabaptist body—and now America's largest such group—originated with the congregations established by Menno Simons (1496–1561) in Germany and the Netherlands. Groups from the Lower Rhine Valley first migrated to Pennsylvania in 1683, settling at Germantown and founding a church there in 1708. Philadelphia's commercial growth drove them westward to the rural isolation of Lancaster County, and from there they spread with other German groups southward into Virginia and the Carolinas. By the early 19th century, they had moved into

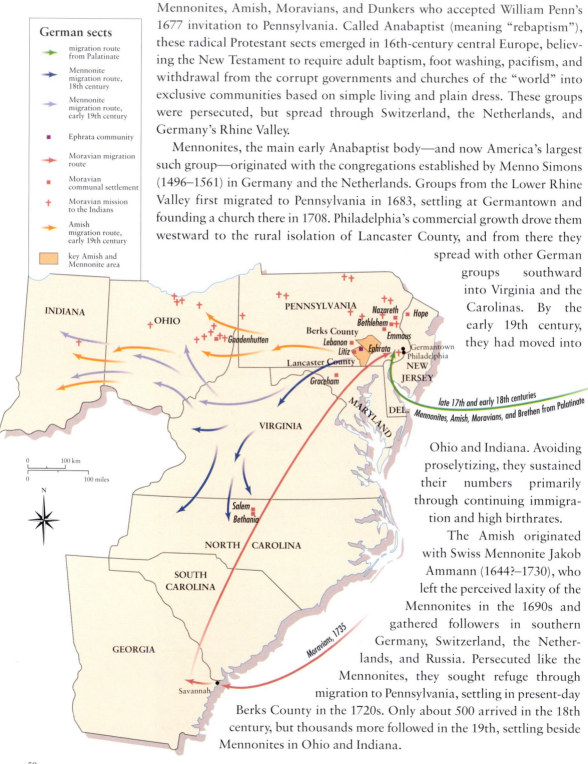

German sects

- ➤ migration route from Palatinate
- ➤ Mennonite migration route, 18th century
- ➤ Mennonite migration route, early 19th century
- ■ Ephrata community
- ➤ Moravian migration route
- ■ Moravian communal settlement
- ✦ Moravian mission to the Indians
- ➤ Amish migration route, early 19th century
- ▇ key Amish and Mennonite area

late 17th and early 18th centuries
Mennonites, Amish, Moravians, and Brethren from Palatinate

Moravians, 1735

Ohio and Indiana. Avoiding proselytizing, they sustained their numbers primarily through continuing immigration and high birthrates.

The Amish originated with Swiss Mennonite Jakob Ammann (1644?–1730), who left the perceived laxity of the Mennonites in the 1690s and gathered followers in southern Germany, Switzerland, the Netherlands, and Russia. Persecuted like the Mennonites, they sought refuge through migration to Pennsylvania, settling in present-day Berks County in the 1720s. Only about 500 arrived in the 18th century, but thousands more followed in the 19th, settling beside Mennonites in Ohio and Indiana.

The Mennonites proved more inclined to modernization and Americanization. The Mennonite Church, the nation's largest Mennonite body, retained pacifism but gradually adopted the church structures, English liturgy, and denominational institutions characteristic of American evangelicalism, spawning several smaller and more conservative schismatic offshoots along the way. The Amish, meanwhile, retained German liturgy, continued to worship in houses or barns rather than erecting churches, and resisted denominational structure. In the 20th century, some moderate Amish began to build meetinghouses and use electricity.

Dunkers (or Brethren), who practiced baptism by triple immersion, originated in the Palatinate when German Reformed began leaving the church to embrace celibacy, Christian communism, and various Anabaptist practices. Their American experience paralleled those of other German sectarians: they were driven by persecution and lured by Pennsylvania, settling in Germantown in 1719 and 1729; they founded their first American congregation in Germantown in 1723; they migrated westward and southward to rural areas; they were rent by progressive-orthodox schisms as they responded in contrasting ways to their new environment; and they eventually formed a single large denomination (the Church of the Brethren) and several smaller, more traditional groups. One important schismatic movement was the Ephrata community, formed in 1732 near what is now Reading, Pennsylvania, and dedicated to celibacy, poverty, and a Saturday Sabbath. It flourished for a time and sent out missionaries to make converts, but internal dissension and tensions with other German sectarians contributed to its 1796 demise. The Brethren more generally evangelistically inclined, grew more rapidly than Mennonites and Amish—and partly at their expense—and formed an Annual Conference in 1742.

Moravians are a missionary and ecumenically inclined group focused in their devotion on the body of Jesus. Their leader, former Lutheran Nikolaus Ludwig von Zinzendorf (1700–60), established a communal village called Hernnhut on his estate in Moravia in 1722 and identified colonial America—especially its German and Indian populations—as a missionary target. Zinzendorf dispatched a group to Georgia in 1735 to establish communal farms and convert the Creeks and Cherokees, but the group relocated to Philadelphia. From that base, they established several Indian missions, founded the First Moravian Church in Philadelphia, and formed several communal settlements, including Bethlehem, Pennsylvania (1741), and Salem (now Winston-Salem), North Carolina (1753). The American settlements maintained ties with Hernnhut and, while adopting some surrounding cultural and social patterns—embracing revivalism and private property, for instance—remained ethnically distinct. Descent rather than conversion became, and remains, the major mechanism by which Moravianism endures.

Maintaining tradition and ethnic identity continues to be both a strength and a problem for these groups, which remain numerically small but fascinating to American outsiders spiritually troubled by modern society.

Catholicism and Judaism in the Colonies

Already by the mid-17th century, incipient Jewish and Catholic communities presaged the later expansion of American religious pluralism beyond Protestantism. Already, too, those communities were being changed by the challenges of American physical and cultural geography: distance from Europe, coastal orientation, river-fed Chesapeake farmlands, and Anglo-Protestant dominance.

Jews settled America as part of a long history of exile, migration, minority status, and intercultural blending. In this case, expulsion by Catholic Spain and Portugal in the 1490s sent them to lives of commerce in such Atlantic seaports as Amsterdam and Recife, Brazil. Portugal's takeover of the latter in 1654 drove twenty-three people from there to New Amsterdam, where their commercial influence prevented their expulsion by the governor. They formed Congregation Shearith Israel in 1656 to meet their religious needs. Two years later, fifteen families from the Netherlands formed another congregation in relatively tolerant Newport, Rhode Island. By the mid-18th century, congregations appeared in other seaports: Savannah (1733), Charleston (1741), and Philadelphia (1745). These early communities consisted largely of Sephardic Jews, whose Iberian experience had generated variations on traditional rituals and a culture combining Hebrew, Spanish, Portuguese, and Muslim elements. Central and eastern European (Ashkenazic) Jews began arriving in the 18th century, becoming a significant presence in Philadelphia and outnumbering Sephardim in New York by 1800.

America was home to approximately 2,000 Jews in 1776. They faced discrimination, but commercial success and distance from European persecution freed them from overt hostility and encouraged interaction with their Christian peers. A more serious challenge was that their small numbers, urban settlement patterns, and colonial isolation from European Jewry left them perennially short of funds, without rabbinical services, and rent by ethnic tensions. Such departures from tradition as increased lay authority, English-language liturgy, and intermarriage with local Protestants resulted. And while Ashkenazim generally acquiesced to Sephardic dominance, sharing American space generated tensions between the two groups, as in a 1738 dispute over the construction of a synagogue in Savannah. Newport's Touro synagogue, constructed in 1763, embodied an emerging dilemma of American Jewish identity: its interior was traditionally orthodox while its simple exterior suggested the home of a prosperous colonial merchant.

Catholicism was a target of persecution in Protestant England, but the well-connected Catholic Calvert family secured colonial havens, first in 1621 on Newfoundland's Avalon peninsula, and then, after Avalon filled with Protestants, on a tract between Virginia and New Netherland named Maryland after the Catholic wife of King Charles I. In 1634, arriving colonists established their initial settlement, St. Mary's, on the Potomac River. The new colony protected Catholicism by enacting religious toleration, and its landowning and officeholding elite was at first largely Catholic. Catholic religious life there was vital, with Jesuits offering regular catechisms, delivering Sunday sermons, erecting chapels, and opening schools and Indian missions. But migrating Puritans and other Protestants soon outnumbered Catholics—who constituted 25 percent of Maryland's population by 1641 but only 9 percent by 1708—and challenged Catholic rule. The Calverts were overthrown temporarily in 1654 amid Puritan hegemony in England, and permanently in 1691, after the Glorious Revolution. Anglicanism then became Maryland's established religion, and by 1750 there were three times as many Anglican as there were Catholic congregations in Maryland. Still, the Catholic presence—including gentry, indentured servants, and slaves, English, Irish, and African—remained more substantial there than in any other English colony, and Maryland continued to be the center of American Catholicism well into the 19th century.

Tolerant Pennsylvania attracted substantial numbers of German and Irish Catholics and—again thanks to Jesuit activity—became the only colony besides Maryland to develop stable Catholic institutions. By 1733, a small Jesuit chapel in Philadelphia catered to a diverse urban group of German, Indian, and (after 1755) French Catholics, and Jesuits opened rural missions for

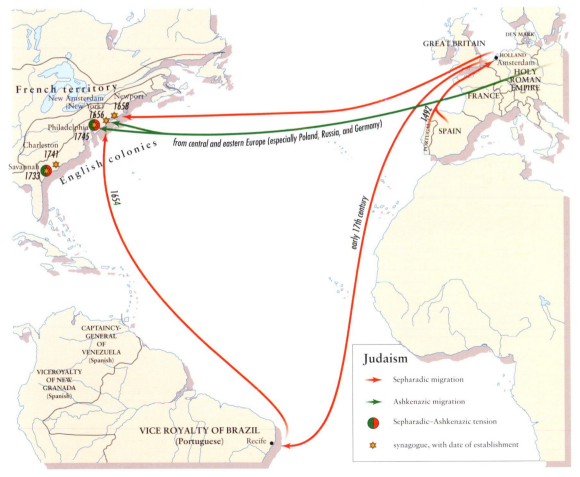

Germans at Reading, Conewago, Goshenhoppen, and Lancaster. Pennsylvania's Catholic population was second only to Maryland's by 1750, but it remained small (about 3 percent in 1765) and ethnically divided. Elsewhere in the colonies, official hostility prevented Catholics from creating lasting institutions. They avoided Puritan New England, where they were denied religious freedom and numbered only 600 by 1785. There were also few in the South. In New York, a brief period of toleration in the 1680s allowed Jesuit missionaries to open a chapel at Fort

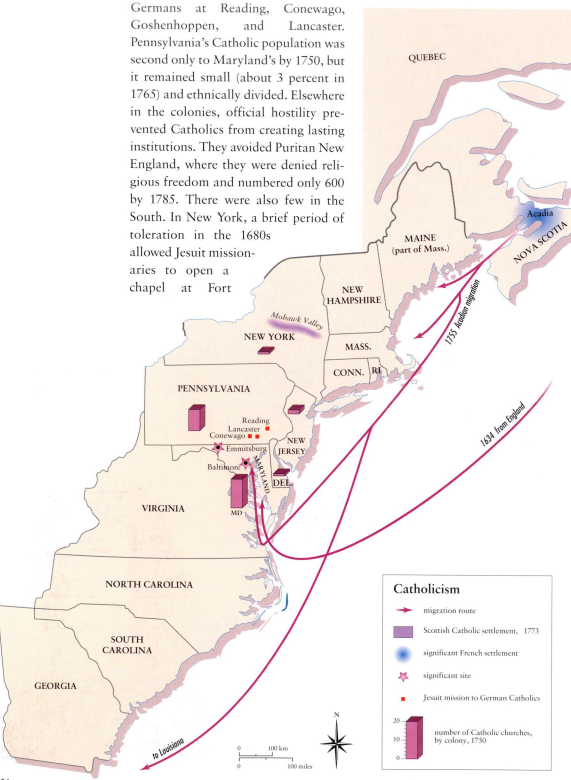

QUEBEC

Acadia

MAINE
(part of Mass.)

NOVA SCOTIA

1755 Acadian migration

Mohawk Valley

NEW HAMPSHIRE

NEW YORK

MASS.

CONN. RI

PENNSYLVANIA

1634 from England

Reading
Lancaster
Conewago

Emmitsburg

Baltimore

NEW JERSEY

MARYLAND

DEL.

VIRGINIA

MD

NORTH CAROLINA

SOUTH CAROLINA

GEORGIA

to Louisiana

Catalicism / Catholicism

Catholicism

→ migration route

Scottish Catholic settlement, 1773

significant French settlement

✶ significant site

■ Jesuit mission to German Catholics

number of Catholic churches, by colony, 1750
20
10
0

N

0   100 km
0   100 miles

James and a school, but this period ended with the Glorious Revolution. Still, New York remained a cosmopolitan colony and continued to attract a multiethnic Catholic population.

America's 25,000 Catholics continued to face Protestant mistrust on the eve of the American Revolution, but Catholic participation in the Continental Congress and the nation's alliance with France improved Catholicism's public image, and independence stimulated its organizational life. In Baltimore, America's first diocese was established in 1789, Mount Saint Mary's Seminary opened in 1791, and a cathedral was constructed in 1804; its Roman architecture declared both its Catholic and republican identities. A few years later, American nuns established the Sisters of Charity in Emmitsburg, Maryland.

As the 19th century dawned, American Jews and Catholics were small but firmly rooted communities, facing a future of ethnic multiplicity and adaptation to Protestant dominance.

NEWFOUNDLAND

Avalon colony

MAINE
(part of Mass.)

NEW HAMPSHIRE

NEW YORK

MASSACHUSETTS

CONNECTICUT RI

Catholic churches as a percent of all churches, by colony, 1750

- 16
- 10
- 0.5
- 0

PENNSYLVANIA

NEW JERSEY

MARYLAND

DELAWARE

VIRGINIA

NORTH CAROLINA

SOUTH CAROLINA

GEORGIA

N

0   100 km

0   100 miles

Cecilius Calvert. The Catholic Calvert family established Maryland in 1634 as a haven for Roman Catholics, and until 1691 wielded political power there.

The Great Awakening

The Great Awakening, America's first major religious revival, was the most important religious event of the colonial period. Rocking the Atlantic seaboard in the middle decades of the 18th century, it established revivalism and emotional conversion as central features of American religious life, lowered denominational boundaries, challenged traditional social patterns, and generated perceptions and conflicts that would inform the American Revolution.

The Awakening resulted from the colonial importation of Pietism, a German movement of the late seventeenth and early eighteenth centuries that emphasized intense, personal, "experiential" contact with God. Pietism strongly influenced British and Dutch religious cultures and crossed the Atlantic between the 1680s and 1730s with German, Scottish, and Scotch-Irish migration. It powerfully influenced a changing provincial social geography in which the dominant and mutually supporting churches and elites of established coastal areas faced a growing challenge from the proliferation of new and more egalitarian frontier communities.

The first manifestations of the Awakening appeared among Pietists in the middle colonies in the 1720s. In the Delaware Valley, Irish Presbyterian immigrant William Tennent Sr. spread a fervent experiential piety and trained like-minded ministers—most notably his son, Gilbert—at his "log college" in Neshaminy, Pennsylvania. Conrad Beissel (1692–1768) arrived in Germantown in 1712 and, beginning in 1722, inspired revivals among recently arrived German Dunkers. In New Jersey's Raritan Valley, Dutch Reformed minister Theodore Frelinghuysen (1691–1748) presided over several revivals in his congregations. The aggressive preaching of Congregationalist Solomon Stoddard (1643–1729) in Northampton, in the Massachusetts backcountry, produced a series of small revivals among his congregation in the early eighteenth century. His grandson, Jonathan Edwards (1703–58), replaced him and, from 1734 through the early 1740s, produced emotional conversions first at Northampton and then in frontier towns throughout the Connecticut Valley with such sensually evocative Calvinist sermons as "Sinners in the Hands of an Angry God," in which he compared sinners to a spider hanging by a thread over a fire.

These local episodes were transformed into a major intercolonial event by the sensational tour of Anglican evangelist George Whitefield (1714–1770). He arrived in October 1739, his growing fame, his integrity, and his combination of Anglicanism, Pietism, and Calvinism enhancing his appeal and earning him the respect if not always enthusiastic support of settled ministers. He preached over the following fifteen months from Savannah, Georgia to York, Maine, in churches and outdoors, sometimes in defiance of local clergy, and often to crowds of unprecedented size—sometimes more than 20,000 people. His greatest successes came in New England—where he spent the fall of 1740—but by the time he left for England in January 1741, his renown, charismatic and controversial preaching, and itinerancy had generated religious excitement and fueled revivalism throughout the colonies.

Other evangelists, some less temperate, followed as the Awakening peaked in the late 1730s and early 1740s. Firebrand Gilbert Tennent left New Jersey in 1741 to retrace Whitefield's steps in New England; in that same year, the even more rabid Long Island preacher James Davenport (1716–1757) brought the enthusiasm to fever pitch in Connecticut and Massachusetts. In Pennsylvania, German Moravian leader Nikolaus Ludwig von Zinzendorf (1700–1760) arrived in 1741 for a visit of several months, bringing revival energy to its height and promoting ecumenical evangelicalism among the region's German Pietists.

The Awakening was initially most effective in the middle and Northern colonies, where the fires of revival began to cool by the mid-1740s. It developed only later and more slowly in the South—despite Whitefield's large audiences in Savannah and Charleston—stifled by unsympathetic Anglican establishments and diffuse settlement patterns. But itinerants working there in the late 1740s and 1750s solidified the Awakening. Samuel Davies (1723–1761) and other log college graduates carried New Side Presbyterianism into Virginia, though his call to the presidency of Princeton in 1759 left the leadership of Southern revivalism to the Separate

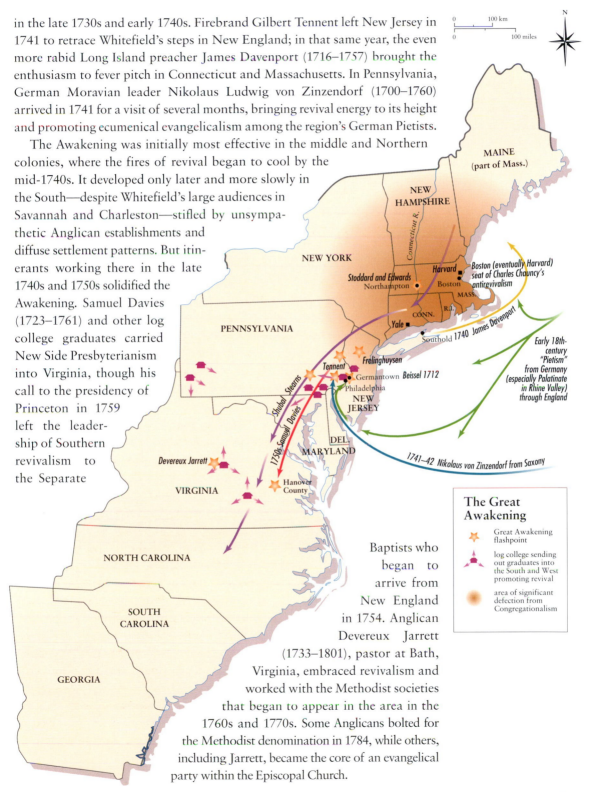

Baptists who began to arrive from New England in 1754. Anglican Devereux Jarrett (1733–1801), pastor at Bath, Virginia, embraced revivalism and worked with the Methodist societies that began to appear in the area in the 1760s and 1770s. Some Anglicans bolted for the Methodist denomination in 1784, while others, including Jarrett, became the core of an evangelical party within the Episcopal Church.

The Great Awakening

⭐ Great Awakening flashpoint

♣ log college sending out graduates into the South and West promoting revival

● area of significant defection from Congregationalism

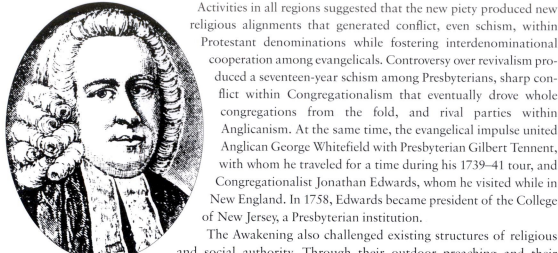

George Whitefield. His electrifying tour of the colonies in 1739–41 fueled the Great Awakening and established revivalism in American religious life.

Activities in all regions suggested that the new piety produced new religious alignments that generated conflict, even schism, within Protestant denominations while fostering interdenominational cooperation among evangelicals. Controversy over revivalism produced a seventeen-year schism among Presbyterians, sharp conflict within Congregationalism that eventually drove whole congregations from the fold, and rival parties within Anglicanism. At the same time, the evangelical impulse united Anglican George Whitefield with Presbyterian Gilbert Tennent, with whom he traveled for a time during his 1739–41 tour, and Congregationalist Jonathan Edwards, whom he visited while in New England. In 1758, Edwards became president of the College of New Jersey, a Presbyterian institution.

The Awakening also challenged existing structures of religious and social authority. Through their outdoor preaching and their emphasis on regeneration rather than formal training and ordination as the key qualification for spiritual authority, itinerant evangelists, often (but by no means always) uneducated, unordained, and uninvited, undermined both confidence in the settled local ministers whom they challenged and defied, and traditional patterns of deference to local elites. This potential—which excited audiences while irking colonial religious establishments—was particularly apparent in Gilbert Tennent's caustic sermon "The Dangers of an Unconverted Ministry" and the activities of James Davenport, a Yale graduate whose extreme methods eventually led to his expulsion from both Connecticut and Massachusetts. The revivals appealed to men and women of every region, class, and Protestant denomination, but their egalitarian and antiauthoritarian thrust was especially popular in interior rural regions, where they reinforced localist values, exacerbated developing tensions between town and country, and augmented the ranks of New Side Presbyterians, New Light Congrgationalists, Separate Baptists, and Methodists.

Critics of the Awakening, concentrated in the cosmopolitan coastal towns, decried what they considered the revivalists' unbridled "enthusiasm," heedless endangerment of tradition, and threat to social order. Perhaps the most outspoken was Congregational minister Charles Chauncy of Boston's First Church, who saw in revivalism an unhealthy elevation of emotion over reason. In 1744 the faculty of Harvard College issued a denunciation of George Whitefield, who had just returned for a second tour. Jonathan Edwards, meanwhile, defended the religious "affections" and produced in the 1740s and 1750s a series of treatises developing a new and influential evangelical Calvinist theology. His alma mater, Yale, became and remained for several decades a focus for the further development of Edwards's "new divinity."

Historians have offered different dates for the end of the Awakening: the late 1740s, by which time its peak of visibility had passed; the late 1750s, when Edwards died (1758), the Presbyterians reunited (1758), and the French and

Indian war stifled frontier revivalism; and the 1770s, when looming political revolution overshadowed spiritual matters. Others have suggested that its aftershocks continued through the late eighteenth century and flowed into a new wave of revivalism—the Second Great Awakening—that began in the late 1790s. Whatever the case, it had profound effects on American religion, society, and politics. An extended and multiethnic intercolonial event, it produced among the American people, particularly Protestants, a new sense of cohesiveness. A popular democratic movement, it broadcast a message of spiritual equality that eroded older religious, social, and political traditions, reinforced the developing republican ideology of self-government and individual rights, and energized rising challenges to colonial religious establishments. A religious impulse at least as much experiential as doctrinal, it promoted ecumenical cooperation and established the evangelical culture that has ever since been central to American Protestantism. The impulses of the Great Awakening, in twilight at the time of independence, were absorbed into the mainstream of American life.

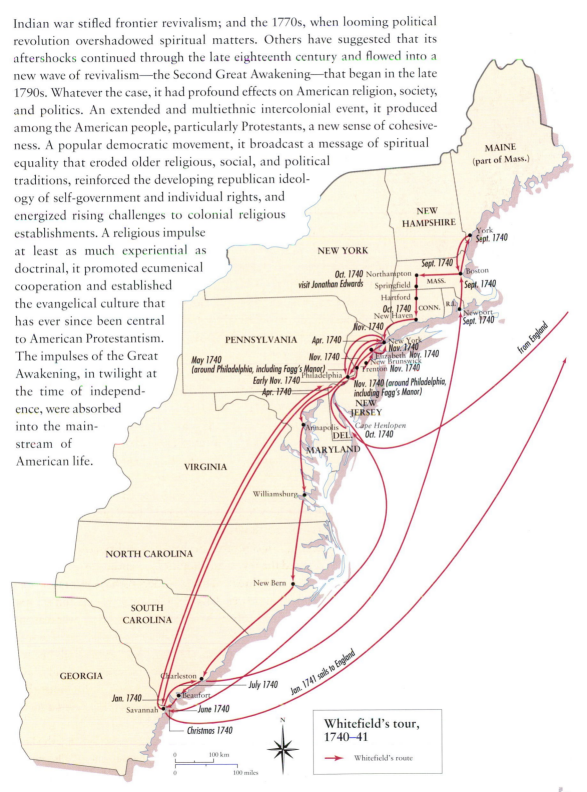

Whitefield's tour, 1740–41

→ Whitefield's route

PART IV: PROTESTANT EXPANSION IN THE NINETEENTH CENTURY

During the decades after 1790, white Americans moved westward from Virginia and the Carolinas into Kentucky, Tennessee, Alabama, and Mississippi, and, in a "Yankee exodus," from New England into New York state, northern Pennsylvania, northern Ohio, and beyond. Euro-Americans settled most of the area east of the Mississippi River by 1830 and began to move west of the Mississippi and to the Pacific coast by 1850. Meanwhile, expanding transportation systems, the commercialization of agriculture, and the onset of industrial production stimulated urban growth, particularly in the Northeast and Midwest. Combined with religious disestablishment under the Constitution, enacted in 1789, these geographic developments left religious groups scrambling, sometimes competitively and sometimes cooperatively, to attract membership in the growing cities and in the newly opening regions of the West. The result was considerable innovation, experimentation, and diversification—in a word, expansion—in American Protestantism.

Revivalism was perhaps the most important tool for addressing the new conditions. Made a central feature of American religious life by a Second Great Awakening, its use sparked among denominations embracing it (especially the Baptists and Methodists) spectacular nationwide growth unmatched by those that did not (Congregationalists, Episcopalians, and Lutherans). Revivalism took different forms in different regions—more sober in the established towns of New England, more boisterous among the dispersed and socially isolated settlers of the West—but everywhere its aim was to enhance religious commitment amid rapid and sometimes disorienting change.

An anxious concern to Protestantize the nation, particularly its urban and Western frontiers, drove American religious leaders in the East—especially in New England—to promote and sponsor organized benevolent and missionary activities. They reached out with similar intent to other regions of the world. Their institutional apparatus became so massive and indicative of Protestant dominance in America that historians have dubbed it a "Protestant Empire," "Benevolent Empire," and "United Evangelical Front." Dominated by Congregationalists and Presbyterians but also including Methodists, and other groups, its combined budget was larger than the federal government's by 1840.

General westward migration pattern, late 18th and early 19th century

The goal of this "empire" was to transform America and the world into the Christian utopia forecast in the Bible—the millennium. It was, many Americans believed, the nation's "manifest destiny" to expand American Protestantism and republicanism across the North American continent to the Pacific—including Indians, Catholics, and Africans, sometimes viewed by white Protestants as potential obstacles—and then, perhaps, to the rest of the globe. Eastern religious leaders deemed California's strategic Pacific location especially important to this effort.

Religious freedom and open space allowed Americans to envision and pursue their religious ideals in varying ways. Some embraced notions of human perfectibility and developed radical movements to accelerate the process. Others developed new liberal theologies based on the divine potential of the individual. Still others combined Christianity with Asian ideas or rejected Christianity altogether. Energized by a sense of new beginnings, some rejected all existing churches and attempted to restore what they considered Christianity's original purity, and others rejected urban life, commercial and industrial capitalism, and conventional social arrangements in favor of religiously inspired communal experiments in rural areas and on the Western perimeter. Again California assumed special prominence, for the inability of the Eastern-based "evangelical empire" to assume tight control over it made it attractive to those pursuing religious alternatives.

Religious Americans of the 19th century diversified Protestantism tremendously and in some cases ventured beyond it, but in all cases they identified their visions with their hope for the expanding young nation.

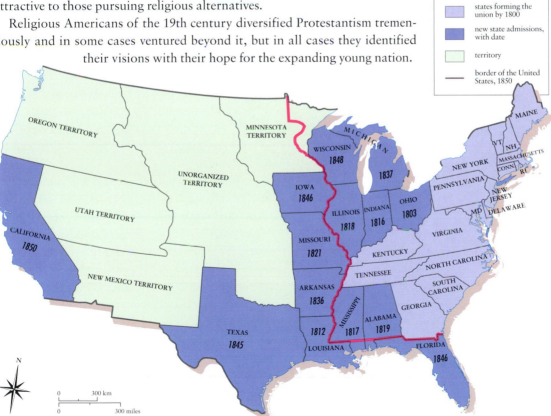

New states admitted to the union, 1800–50

— border of the United States, 1800

  states forming the union by 1800

  new state admissions, with date

  territory

— border of the United States, 1850

The Second Great Awakening

Between the 1790s and the 1830s a nationwide series of religious revivals called the Second Great Awakening established revivalism as a fixture of American religion and became intertwined with the westward expansion of the new nation.

The Awakening began in rural Connecticut and New Hampshire in the late 1790s, becoming an especially powerful force in New England after Yale College students attended revivals in 1801—about a third of the student body converted—and went on as ministers to spread revivalism throughout the region's Congregational churches over the following two decades. New England revivalism was generally sedate and conservative, producing a host of regional missionary, benevolent, and moral reform associations designed to shore up faltering Congregational establishments and to extend their middle-class values into new Western settlements. Revival-energized Yale and Andover seminary graduates accompanied the westward "Yankee migration" into New York State and Ohio as missionaries and educators, and Congregationalists and Presbyterians pooled their resources in an 1801 "Plan of Union" to facilitate the founding of churches and schools there. As a result, churches of both denominations multiplied from New York and northern Ohio to Wisconsin and Minnesota.

A second and more boisterous phase of the Awakening occurred among the growing number of Americans—particularly Methodists, Baptists, and Scotch-Irish Presbyterians from western Virginia and the Carolinas—crossing the Cumberland Gap into trans-Appalachian Kentucky and Tennessee in the 1790s. Arriving in southwestern Kentucky in 1796, Scotch-Irish Presbyterian James McGready (1758–1817) and some North Carolina Methodists conducted revivals in 1799 and 1800 at his Muddy River, Red River, and Gaspar River parishes. With him at Gaspar River was Presbyterian Barton Stone (1772–1844), pastor at western Kentucky's Concord and Cane Ridge churches, who arranged what became a massive "camp meeting" at Cane Ridge in 1801. The 10,000 people who attended this emotional weeklong "Great Revival" included Presbyterian, Baptist, and Methodist preachers, who proceeded over the following three years to hold camp meetings across Kentucky, Tennessee, and southern Ohio. Well adapted to the sparsely settled Western frontier, such meetings effectively spread Protestant Christianity throughout the region, stimulated the formation of cohesive religious communities, and propelled such denominations as the Baptists and Methodists to national dominance. (Eastern Presbyterian authorities soon condemned the revivals, slowing their Western growth and driving prorevival elements in Tennessee to form the schismatic Cumberland Presbyterian Church in 1810.)

A third and final phase was centered in New York, a newly opening and rapidly developing region populated largely by the "Yankee migration." There, Charles Grandison Finney (1792–1875) and others conducted revivals through the 1820s and early 1830s, contributing to a culture of evangelicalism, moral reform, and radical social and religious experimentation so intense—and made more so by the powerful economic and social impact of the new Erie Canal (1825)—that western New York came to be called the "burned-over district." The region gave birth to Mormonism, Spiritualism, and the women's rights movement, and became a stronghold of Shakerism, abolitionism, and various communitarian movements.

If the revivals subsided, their effects did not. All three phases of the Awakening profoundly and lastingly shaped the religious and cultural life of the young nation.

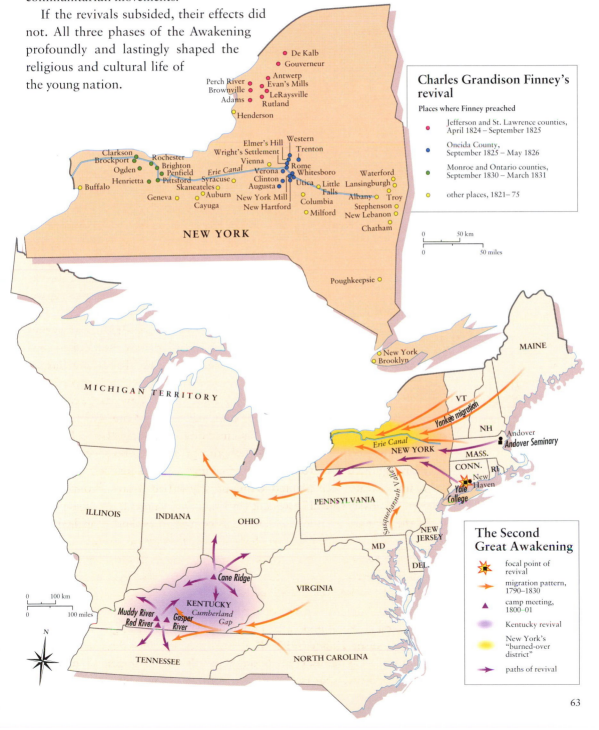

Charles Grandison Finney's revival

Places where Finney preached

- ● Jefferson and St. Lawrence counties, April 1824 – September 1825
- ● Oneida County, September 1825 – May 1826
- ● Monroe and Ontario counties, September 1830 – March 1831
- ● other places, 1821– 75

The Second Great Awakening

- ✴ focal point of revival
- → migration pattern, 1790–1830
- ▲ camp meeting, 1800–01
- ● Kentucky revival
- ● New York's "burned-over district"
- → paths of revival

The Baptists and Methodists Surge

Methodists

■ college or university

Number of Methodists,
by conference, 1844,
in thousands

3   20   40   60 73

Energized by the Second Great Awakening, and using revivalism and other methods well suited to geographic expansion, the Baptist and Methodist denominations experienced phenomenal growth, especially in the West, and became by far the new nation's largest.

The Methodists owed much of their growth to camp meetings in the West and urban revivals in the East, both of which they gradually institutionalized as regular parts of Methodist life. But equally important was the Church's combination of a tightly centralized national structure with a "circuit" system (operational by the 1790s) that allowed a small number of itinerant ministers to serve the vast spaces of the Western frontier. Traveling hundreds and thousands of miles on horseback, preachers like Peter Cartwright (1785–1872) formed lay-conducted "classes" for worship, prayer, and Bible study and left these in the hands of lay leaders between visits. As Western settlements grew, these groups evolved into congregations, constructing churches and becoming integrated into the national denominational hierarchy as circuits were combined into territorial districts and regional annual conferences under the governance of the national quadrennial General Conference. Methodism also expanded, numerically and geographically, through the proliferation of Sunday schools, mission stations, and such colleges as Asbury in Maryland (1816) and Wesleyan in Connecticut (1831). It expanded ethnically as pietistic German-American converts in Pennsylvania and Maryland founded the United Brethren in Christ in 1800 and the Evangelical Association in 1803, both of which later merged with the Methodist church. Methodism's growth was hardly smooth—opposition to bishops' authority sparked the formation of the Republican Methodist Church (1794) and Protestant Methodist Church (1830), African-Americans were driven by discrimination to form separate denominations, and sectional tensions split the church into northern and southern branches in 1844—but its expansion from fewer than 65,000 adherents in 1800 to more than 1 million by 1850 made it twice the size of any other American denomination.

Baptist growth, too, was spectacular. Having spread along the Southern frontier during and after the first Great Awakening, Baptists crossed the Appalachians by the 1770s and joined Methodists in the Great Revival. Their congregationalism, absence of centralized structure, and reliance on "farmer-preachers" who moved with advancing settlement allowed a flexibility well suited to the migratory nature and social fluidity of frontier life. Unhindered by organizational hierarchies, Baptists easily formed churches and conducted "protracted meetings" that lasted for several days, during which many converts were won. They became especially numerous in the South. Baptists also expanded through the institutions of the "Evangelical Empire," forming denominational missionary and tract societies and joining other frontier denominations in ecumenical endeavors. They also founded several colleges. Like the Methodists, they experienced internal division: small groups opposed to revivalism kept their distance from the majority; Southern and Western groups resisted the ecumenism, missionary outreach, and institutional network of Northeastern Baptists; and the slavery controversy generated a permanent sectional split in 1845. But numbering nearly 600,000 (North and South) by midcentury, they were the nation's second-largest Protestant group, trailing only the Methodists.

The expansion of Methodism and Baptism during the early 19th century bears powerful witness to the interplay between geography and religion in the new nation.

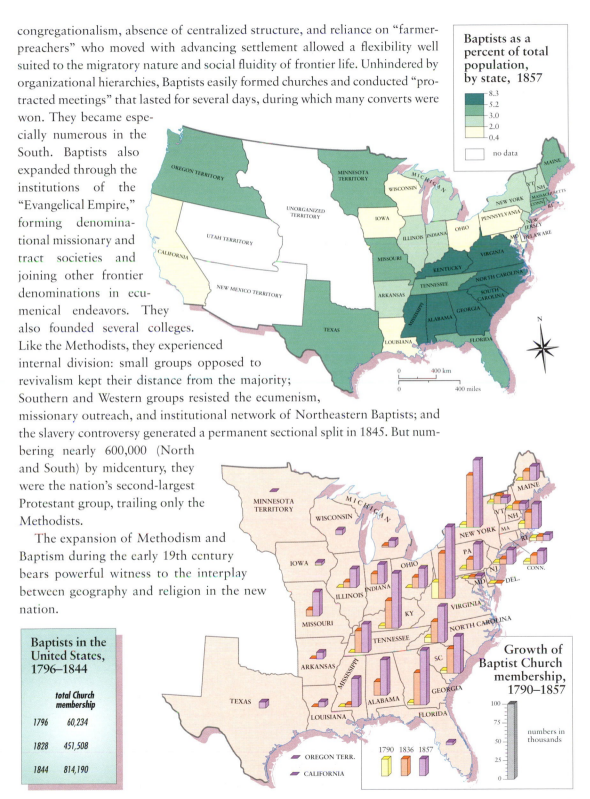

Baptists as a percent of total population, by state, 1857

- 8.3
- 5.2
- 3.0
- 2.0
- 0.4
- no data

Growth of Baptist Church membership, 1790–1857

numbers in thousands

1790 1836 1857

■ OREGON TERR.
■ CALIFORNIA

Baptists in the United States, 1796–1844

	total Church membership
1796	60,234
1828	451,508
1844	814,190

Missionary Outreach

The Protestant empire was above all a missionary enterprise intended by its promoters to transform and sacralize the American landscape in their image. Its leaders—white middle-class Northeasterners, New Englanders in particular—anxiously sought to expand their religious influence to peoples socially, culturally, and geographically distant from the centers of their civilization.

They found precedent in the London Missionary Society, formed in 1795 to evangelize India, but their primary engines were local. The Second Great Awakening generated evangelical zeal, encouraged social service, promoted revivalism as a means of spreading Christianity, and spawned an array of inter-denominational organizations to carry out the missionary enterprise and hasten the millennium. The ideology of manifest destiny promised that God had chosen the United States to occupy the continent and extend Protestant culture to non-Christian peoples in North America and around the world. This ideology derived in large part from American Puritanism, and it is therefore no coincidence that, while the national offices of the Benevolent Empire were in New York and Philadelphia, the primary missionary impulse came from New England. A third stimulus was the anxiety with which Protestant expansionists viewed the "wild" urban and Western frontiers—both particular targets of their benevolence.

Missionary activism appeared at the state level as early as the 1790s, when societies were founded in New York (1796), Connecticut (1798), and Massachusetts (1799) to form churches and schools among whites in the seaboard cities and the trans-Appalachian West. The Connecticut and Massachusetts societies were invigorated after Congregationalists and Presbyterians there joined forces in an 1801 Plan of Union. By 1826, accelerating white Western settlement and expanding missionary outreach had led to the establishment in New York City of a consolidated national organization, the American Home Mission Society (AHMS). Six years later, Baptists formed the American Baptist Home Mission Society (ABHMS), also in New York. Reaching as far as Oregon and California, AHMS and ABHMS missionaries helped develop Eastern Protestant institutions and culture throughout the West through their preaching, teaching, and civic service. Also contributing to the urban and westward reach of the Protestant Empire were the American Bible Society, the American Tract Society, and the American Sunday School Union, and in particular evangelical women, who staffed Eastern voluntary societies and, on occasion, married male missionaries in order to serve farther afield.

Missionary work among Native Americans—by now increasingly wary of white expansionism and protective of their traditional cultures—produced limited results. The most significant efforts were sponsored by the American Board of Commissioners for Foreign Missions (ABCFM), a Congregationalist-Presbyterian society established in 1810. Promoting Anglo-American agriculture and domesticity as well as Christianity, its agents were most effective among the Cherokees of eastern Tennessee, western North Carolina, and northern Georgia. Arriving in 1825 and supported in part by the federal gov-

ABCFM missions to the Indians	
tribe	number of missions
Cherokees	154
Choctaws	130
Osages	44
New-York Indians	33
Ojibwas	27
Mackinaw	27
Chickasaws	17
Sioux	16
Oregon Indians	13
Stockbridge Indians	10
Maumee	7
Pawnees	6
Creeks	5
Abernaquis	1
total	490

ernment's "civilization fund," ABCFM missionary Samuel A. Worcester (1798–1859) and New England-educated Native American minister Elias Boudinot (b. Galegina; 1803?–39) persuaded many Cherokees to accept Protestantism, whites' agricultural and political patterns, and a written version of the Cherokee language. The federal government nonetheless removed the tribe in the 1830s to Oklahoma, where Worcester joined them. Similarly, the ABCFM's Stephen R. Riggs (1812–83) and his wife Mary worked among Minnesota's Dakota (Sioux) beginning in 1837, learning their language, converting several to Christianity, settled agriculture, private property, and literacy, and erecting the Hazelwood mission in 1856. But warfare between non-Christian Dakotas and the federal government soon drove Riggs and the Dakota Christians westward into what is now South Dakota.

Catholic missionaries, too, missionized Western natives. The most notable was Belgian Jesuit Pierre-Jean De Smet (1801–73), who arrived in the United States in 1821 and left St. Louis in 1840 to work among the Flathead or Salish of Montana's Bitterroot Valley. His St. Mary's mission, established in 1841 near Missoula, was soon staffed by several clergy and nuns, although his frequent trips to Europe to garner support kept him from spending much time there himself. St. Mary's was followed by other Jesuit missions in the Columbia and Willamette river valleys (some of which De Smet helped to found) and by Jesuit activity among the Blackfoot and Dakota. But growing Indian hostility in the Northwest and the discovery of gold in California in 1848 prevented large-scale Catholic immigration in the region, and financial difficulty forced De Smet to abandon his mission in 1855.

Missions in the United States, 1817–83

✝ mission

Missionaries' treks

→ De Smet, 1840

→ Lee, 1834

→ Whitmans, 1836

→ Worcester, 1825

→ Riggs, 1837

Borders and states as of 1880

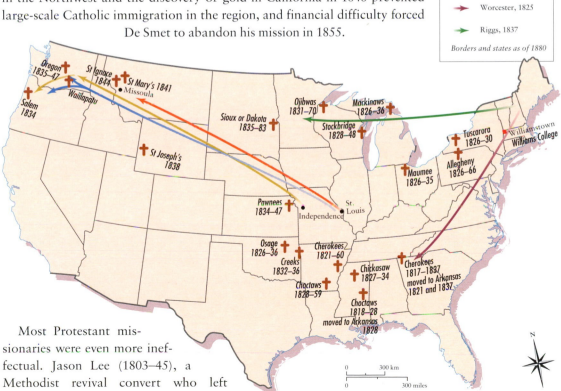

Most Protestant missionaries were even more ineffectual. Jason Lee (1803–45), a Methodist revival convert who left

Henry Opukahaia, the Hawaiian native whose highly publicized visit to New England in 1818 made Hawaii a matter of missionary interest to the ABCFM.

Independence, Missouri, in 1834 to work among the Flatheads of Oregon. He made no converts and his mission failed within a year of his death. More disastrous was the fate of Presbyterians Narcissa (1808–47) and Marcus Whitman (1802–47), who traversed the continent by wagon train and horseback in 1836 and established a mission among the Cayuse at Waiilapatu, only to be massacred at their mission house in 1847. Revitalization religions began to appear among the natives of the Pacific Northwest shortly thereafter.

The Protestant missionary impulse assumed a global thrust in 1806, when a group of revival-energized Williams College students led by Samuel J. Mills (1783–1818) and crouched in a hayloft during a rainstorm spontaneously held the famous "haystack prayer meeting" and pledged their lives to missionizing abroad. The group went on to Andover Seminary, where they were joined by Adoniram Judson (1788–1850). Their efforts produced the ABCFM, which in 1812 sent Judson, his wife Ann (1789–1826), and Luther Rice (1783–1836) to India. The three converted to Baptist belief en route and, while the Judsons established missions in Burma, Bombay, and Ceylon (now Sri Lanka), Rice returned to the United States for a lobbying effort among the Baptists that spurred them to establish their own foreign mission society in 1814. Poor health kept Mills from foreign travel, but he was active nonetheless. He toured the West for the Connecticut and Massachusetts missionary societies in 1812–13 to assess the region's religious needs, and led the ABCFM to reach for the Sandwich Islands (Hawaii) in 1819 by sensationalizing the conversion, 1809 arrival in New England, and death by typhus in 1818 of Hawaiian native Henry Obookiah (Opukahaia). Hoping to begin the millennium on this new Pacific frontier, ABCFM missionaries Hiram Bingham (1789–1869), Asa Thurston (1787–1868), and others, aided by Kamehameha II (Liholiho), converted many islanders and built Congregational churches and schools but did not supplant local tradition. Mills and his colleagues also targeted west Africa, where they hoped to send freed slaves as agents. By midcentury American missionaries were in China, Southeast Asia, Turkey, Palestine, and Latin America, exporting Protestantism in tandem with an expanding American commerce.

The Benevolent Empire as an interdenominational endeavor crumbled by 1850, undermined by sectional conflict and denominational consciousness, and the Civil War severely disrupted missionary outreach. But the missionary impulse survived. Work abroad—this time under denominational auspices and joined by American Catholics—rebounded in the decades after 1880 with the nation's expanding political and economic imperialism in Asia and Latin America. Missionaries also found new fields closer to home. They continued evangelizing Native Americans but also turned after 1865 to the emancipated slave population of the Southern states and the growing numbers of non-Protestant immigrants who came from Europe and Asia to augment an expanding urban-industrial working class. Their fearful concern for the future of Protestant piety, morality, and cultural dominance—not to mention white racial supremacy—in the face of increasing religious and cultural diversity generated schools and colleges among Southern blacks and social programs and urban missions among Northern immigrants. Their message of Protestantism, republicanism, and industrial discipline was often perceived as patronizing and therefore resisted.

In the final analysis, the missionary ideology was most influential among white Protestants themselves. The image of an expansive American Christian culture proved problematic, as liberal Protestants sensitive to cultural imperialism increasingly acknowledged by the 1930s and 1940s. But it has survived among conservative evangelicals and remains fundamental to American domestic and foreign policy.

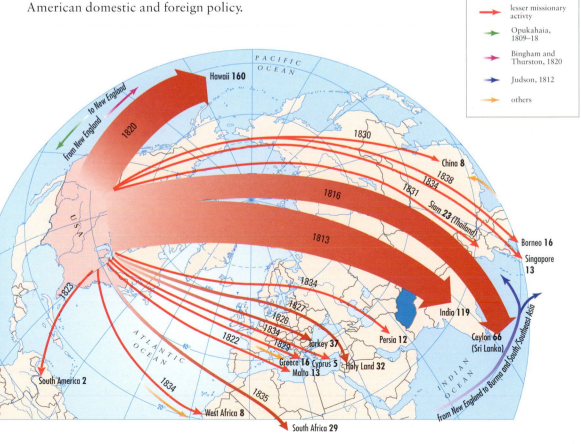

ABCFM missionary activities, 1820–40

- major missionary activity, with numbers shown
- 1820   year of first missionary arrival
- lesser missionary activity
- Opukahaia, 1809–18
- Bingham and Thurston, 1820
- Judson, 1812
- others

Restorationism and the Disciples of Christ

Presbyterian minister Barton Stone. He organized the Cane Ridge revival and led the restorationist "Christian" movement in the trans-Appalachian West.

The sense of new beginnings encouraged by America's revolutionary separation from England and the opening of the trans-Appalachian West to white settlement found religious expression in groups seeking to liberate the original Christianity of New Testament times from subsequent institutional accretions and denominational divisions and restore its "primitive" purity.

Small restorationist groups developed in North Carolina and on the New England frontier in the late 18th and early 19th centuries—coming together by 1820 as the "Christian Connection" and remaining strong in both areas—but the most influential movements of this sort developed west of the Appalachians. In Kentucky, Presbyterian minister and Cane Ridge organizer Barton Stone (1772–1844), alienated from Eastern denominational authorities by tensions over his revivalism and expelled from the Kentucky Synod in 1803, declared the Bible rather than creeds and ecclesiastical hierarchies as his only spiritual guide and formed a religious union under the simple name Christian in 1804. His movement spread among the Presbyterian churches of the Ohio River Valley, embracing about 10,000 "Christians" by 1830. A similar movement began in western Pennsylvania when Scotch-Irish Presbyterian immigrant Thomas Campbell (1763–1854) formed the "Christian Association of Washington County" in 1809 and then, in 1812, joined by his son Alexander (1788–1866), the Brush Run Church. Assuming leadership of the movement, Alexander formed groups called "Disciples of Christ" across the Midwest and upper South, attracting many Baptist congregations with his commitments to adult baptism, congregational polity, and equality of laity and clergy. Campbell's became one of the fastest- growing religious movements of the period, numbering about 12,000 by 1830.

In Lexington, Kentucky, in 1832, Campbell and Stone, joined by several Christian Connection churches, merged their movements into the "Disciples of Christ." The union remained loose, its component congregations protective of their autonomy but united on a platform of anticreedalism, congregationalism, Christian union, and the sole authority of the New Testament. But the movement competed effectively with Baptists and Methodists on the Western frontier as farmer-preachers spread it from Ohio and Kentucky northward into Michigan, Pennsylvania, and New York; eastward into Maryland, Virginia, and the Carolinas; and westward and southward into Indiana, Illinois, Iowa, Wisconsin, Missouri, Arkansas, and Texas. Their growth was dramatic: about 118,000 by 1850, 192,000 by 1860, and 500,000 by the early 1880s. They avoided denominational structure but gradually institutionalized nonetheless, by mid-century holding a national convention in Cincinnati.

By the early 20th century, the tension between local autonomy and primitive purity on the one hand and Christian union on the other led rural, conservative Southern congregations to take the name Church of Christ and separate from

the increasingly urban, institutionalized, theologically
liberal, and ecumenically
inclined Disciples of the
upper Midwest. But the continued growth of both
groups suggests restora-
tionism's enduring appeal.

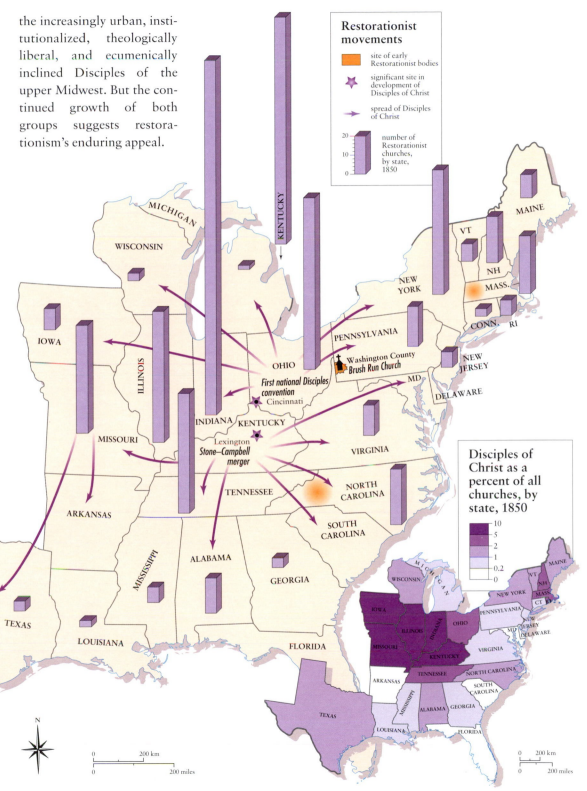

Restorationist movements

- site of early Restorationist bodies
- significant site in development of Disciples of Christ
- spread of Disciples of Christ
- number of Restorationist churches, by state, 1850
  - 20
  - 10
  - 0

First national Disciples convention
• Cincinnati

Washington County
Brush Run Church

Lexington
Stone–Campbell merger

Disciples of Christ as a percent of all churches, by state, 1850

- 10
- 5
- 2
- 1
- 0.2
- 0

0   200 km

0   200 miles

0   200 km

0   200 miles

Unitarians and Universalists

Unitarian churches as a percent of all churches, by state, 1850

- 12
- 3
- 1
- 0.03
- 0

Most major American denominations of the 19th century modified traditional Protestant notions of human depravity and predestination in favor of human ability and free will, but none so thoroughly as Unitarianism, a product of Boston's intellectual culture, and Universalism.

Unitarianism rejects the doctrine of the Trinity in favor of God's oneness. It surfaced periodically through the history of Christianity before appearing in Enlightenment England, becoming official doctrine at Anglican King's Chapel in Boston in 1785, and finding an advocate in British émigré Joseph Priestley (1733–1804), who founded two congregations in Pennsylvania in the 1790s. American Unitarianism originated above all with Congregationalist opponents of the Great Awakening, who rejected its revivalism and orthodoxy in favor of such liberal positions as God's benevolence, Jesus' divine but subordinate status, human moral efficacy, and a rationalistic approach to Scripture.

The embrace of these positions by the professional classes of eastern Massachusetts during the late 18th century generated a rift between orthodox and liberal Congregationalists. Schism ensued when a liberal takeover of Harvard College in 1805 prompted the founding of orthodox Andover Seminary in 1808, William Ellery Channing (1780–1842) asserted "Unitarian Christianity" in a provocative 1819 sermon, and an 1820 Massachusetts Supreme Court decision allowed Unitarians to assume control of some one hundred Congregational parishes in eastern Massachusetts. In 1825, 125 churches, most in and around Boston, formed an informal American Unitarian Association. (A more formal National Conference of Unitarian Churches followed in

Unitarianism and Transcendentalism

- ● Unitarian congregation
- ■ Harvard College, intellectual center of Unitarianism
- ♱ Andover Seminary, founded in response to triumph of Unitarianism at Harvard
- ♰ Unitarian seminary
- → Unitarian expansion
- ▲ site of David Thoreau's Transcendentalist-inspired experiment in solitary living
- ✦ Transcendentalist-inspired communitarian experiment

borders and states as of 1850

1865.) Unitarianism became the dominant church of maritime New England.

Cool toward revivalism and disinclined to proselytize, Unitarians attracted few adherents in other areas. Only three churches were founded in the revival-washed Connecticut Valley by 1850, and westward Yankee migration brought only scattered churches to the larger cities along the way: Buffalo (1831), St. Louis (1834), Chicago (1836), and San Francisco (1850). Nor did its abolitionist associations win it many adherents in the South. California's liberal coastal culture eventually fostered a strong Unitarian presence, but in 1850, 90 percent of the nation's Unitarian churches were in New England. This geographic concentration persists today.

Unitarianism soon spawned an even more liberal offshoot: Transcendentalism, which infused Unitarianism with German idealism and Hindu ideas. In 1836, a Boston-area group led by Ralph Waldo Emerson (1803–82) formed the Transcendental Club, and in 1838 Emerson offered Transcendentalism's manifesto in a commencement address at Harvard Divinity School. Transcendentalism generated the short-lived communal experiments of Brook Farm (1841) and Fruitlands (1843), and inspired Henry David Thoreau's famous 1845 retreat to Walden Pond. It also influenced a range of emerging "metaphysical" movements in American religion.

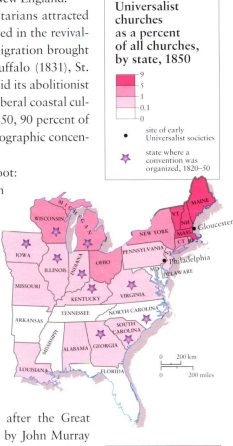

Universalist churches as a percent of all churches, by state, 1850

- 9
- 5
- 1
- 0.1
- 0

• site of early Universalist societies

✶ state where a convention was organized, 1820–50

Universalism teaches that all human beings will achieve salvation. It circulated in post-Reformation England and Germany but was particularly salient in the populist religious subculture that developed in rural northern New England after the Great Awakening. It was spread in the early United States primarily by John Murray (1741–1815) and by Elnahan Winchester (1751–97). Murray preached throughout the Northeast, founding a church in Gloucester, Massachusetts, in 1779 and finally settling in Boston. Winchester worked in the Philadelphia area, attracting several Baptists and in 1781 founding the Society for Universal Baptists. Resistant to centralized organization, American Universalists at first formed scattered societies in the New England and mid-Atlantic states, but a need for legal recognition led them to form regional conventions in New England (1785) and Philadelphia (1790) and eventually, in 1833, the Universalist Church of America. The new denomination remained strongest in New England—where about 55 percent of its churches were located in 1850—but its populist character promoted its spread into the small towns and rural areas of the South and West. Its greatest growth came between 1820 and 1850, when conventions were organized in several Southern and Western states. By 1900 there were about 65,000 Universalists in nearly 1,000 societies.

Universalism growth in the United States, 1840–49

1840
792 societies

1849
1,124 churches or societies, 753 meetinghouses (including those owned in part only)

Doctrinal similarity and declining membership prompted Unitarians and Universalists to merge into the Unitarian Universalist Association in 1961. This organization—small, socially progressive, largely Northeastern, and especially strong among professionals and academics—remains a key religious expression of American liberal impulses.

American Metaphysical Movements

In the Northeast and Midwest, disorientation amid rapid industrialization, urbanization, westward expansion, and the rising authority of science impelled some middle-class Americans of the mid- to late 19th century to explore new spiritual frontiers. Many of the resulting new movements flourished in the dynamic and still unformed culture of California.

The first to emerge was Spiritualism, based on a belief that human mediums could establish scientifically verifiable contact with spirits and transmit religious truth in ritualized séances. Its origins lay in New York's burned-over district, where in 1848 Kate and Margaret Fox of Hydesville claimed to have communicated with spirits through coded knockings. The practice spread from the Northeast and Midwest to California—though less in the South, where it was associated with abolitionism—accompanied by a liberal theology, by visions of eternal progression after death through a hierarchy of "spheres," and by assurances that spirits were working to bolster traditional republican morality and promote social reform in a commercializing society. Spiritualists shunned centralized structures and formal creeds, seeking instead personal growth in small séance groups. But they developed Sunday services in such large cities as New York and Boston, founded a few congregations, and formed short-lived utopian communities at Mountain Cove in western Virginia and Kiantone in western Pennsylvania. They later established communities and camps from New York and Massachusetts to Florida to New Mexico and California, many of which still exist. New York, Chicago, and San Francisco became important centers of activity. In 1893, Spiritualists meeting in Chicago formed the National Spiritualist Association of Churches, now the nation's largest such organization. Other, smaller organizations followed in the 20th century.

Theosophy developed somewhat later, when mystically inclined Russian immigrant Helena Petrovna Blavatsky (1831–91) and Henry Steel Olcott (1832–1907) rejected Spiritualism to pursue deeper metaphysical searching. They formed the Theosophical Society in New York City in 1875, which attracted well-educated and spiritually dissatisfied urbanites by promoting occult knowledge, spiritual growth, universal brotherhood, and Asian religious wisdom through meditative contact with advanced spiritual guides (*Mahatmas*). Blavatsky and Olcott increasingly infused Asian elements into Theosophy after migrating to India in 1878 and converting to Buddhism in Ceylon (Sri Lanka) in 1880. This change prompted the formation of the rival Theosophical Society of America, established in New York in 1895 and later relocated to Pasadena, California. Vigorous Theosophical activity on the West Coast produced the Point Loma colony near San Diego, founded in 1898, and the United Lodge of Theosophists, founded in Los Angeles in 1908. Back East, the original society moved in a Hindu direction, established new headquarters in Wheaton, Illinois, and grew to a membership of about 50,000 in forty countries (10,000 in the United States) by 1930. Theosophy remains small and largely confined to urban elites, but has been a major vehicle for blending Asian and Western traditions in American religious life.

Spiritualism

- ■ utopian community
- ■ spiritualist camp today
- ● other Spiritualism landmark
- ▲ early Spiritualist churches, 1860

Milton — WASHINGTON
WASHINGTON
MONTANA
OREGON
IDAHO
NORTH DAKOTA
MINNESOTA
SOUTH DAKOTA
WISCONSIN
Charlevoix
Bellaire
MICHIGAN
Chippewa Falls
South Branch
MAINE
Madison
Northport
VT
NH
MA
CT
Onset
New London
Essex Co.
Dawn Valcour 1874–75
Hydesville
Geneseo Co.
Lily Dale
NEW YORK
Headquarters of NSAC
Kiantone 1853–63
PENNSYLVANIA
CALIFORNIA
NEVADA
UTAH
WYOMING
IOWA
Clinton
Cherry Valley
Chicago
Huron Co.
ILLINOIS
INDIANA
OHIO
WV
MD
DEL
Fountain Grove 1876–1900
COLORADO
KANSAS
NEBRASKA
MISSOURI
Chesterfield
KENTUCKY
VIRGINIA
Mountain Cove 1851–53
Escondito
ARIZONA
NEW MEXICO
OKLAHOMA
ARKANSAS
TENNESSEE
NORTH CAROLINA
SOUTH CAROLINA
Tonopah
Shalam Colony 1884–1901
TEXAS
Hico
MISSISSIPPI
ALABAMA
GEORGIA
LOUISIANA
FLORIDA
Cassadaga

N

| 0 | 300 km |
| 0 | 300 miles |

Penobscot Co.
MAINE
Hancock Co.
VT
Knox Co.
NH
Windsor Co.
Strafford Co.
Essex Co.
MA
Middlesex Co.
Hartford Co.
CT
Providence Co.
Windham Co.
RI

Spiritualist periodicals, 1847–1900

Number of periodicals, per town

- ● 2
- ● 3
- ● 4
- ● 5
- ● 6
- ● 7
- ● 1
- ● 13
- ● 21
- ● 26
- ● 27

WASHINGTON
Portland
OREGON
MONTANA
NORTH DAKOTA
MINNESOTA
SOUTH DAKOTA
WISCONSIN
MICHIGAN
Sandusky
Auburn
NEW YORK
VT
NH
MAINE
Boston
MA
Hopedale
CT
IDAHO
WYOMING
IOWA
Chicago
ILLINOIS
INDIANA
OHIO
Berlin Heights
Cleveland
PENNSYLVANIA
Lily Dale
Philadelphia
Brooklyn
New York
CALIFORNIA
NEVADA
UTAH
COLORADO
NEBRASKA
Sacramento
San Francisco
KANSAS
Topeka
MISSOURI
St.Louis
Springfield
Cincinnati
WEST VIRGINIA
Washington
VIRGINIA
KENTUCKY
NORTH CAROLINA
ARIZONA
NEW MEXICO
OKLAHOMA
ARKANSAS
TENNESSEE
Memphis
SOUTH CAROLINA
GEORGIA
Atlanta
ALABAMA
MISSISSIPPI
TEXAS
Waco
Hempstead
LOUISIANA
New Orleans
FLORIDA

N

| 0 | 300 km |
| 0 | 300 miles |

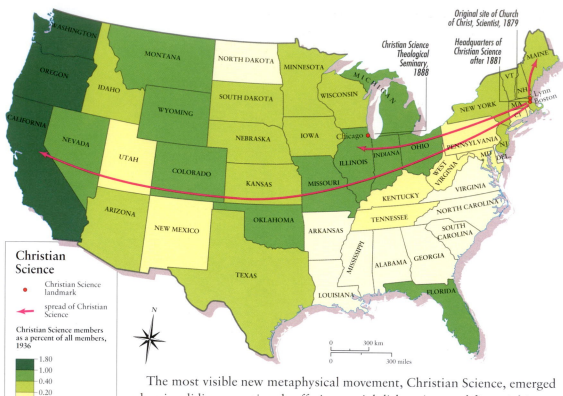

Original site of Church
of Christ, Scientist, 1879

Christian Science
Theological
Seminary,
1888

Headquarters of
Christian Science
after 1881

Christian Science

• Christian Science landmark

← spread of Christian Science

Christian Science members
as a percent of all members,
1936

- 1.80
- 1.00
- 0.40
- 0.20
- 0.11
- 0.02

Christian Science in the United States

1906
636 churches
(0.3 % of all churches)

1936
1970 churches
(0.9 % of all churches)

1990
1862 churches
(0.7 % of all churches)

The most visible new metaphysical movement, Christian Science, emerged when invalidism, emotional suffering, social dislocation, and financial instability led New Hampshire Congregationalist Mary Baker Eddy (1821–1910) to seek personal spiritual power. Her sudden recovery from a fall prompted her to develop a religious system based on the convictions that disease, death, evil, and matter were illusory, that Jesus' love is the only reality, that belief in this truth brings health and redemption, and that Jesus had developed "scientific" healing methods. She established the Church of Christ, Scientist in Lynn, Massachusetts, in 1879 and in 1881 founded the Massachusetts Metaphysical College, from which her students, mostly socially marginalized working-class urban women, spread to cities across the nation as "practitioners." As the movement expanded geographically, increased numerically, and attracted members of prestige and wealth, Eddy developed a tightly centralized bureaucratic structure, relocating to Boston and reorganizing the Boston church as the First Church of Christ, Scientist in 1892. It became and remains the movement's headquarters. Chicago became an important secondary center. The church grew quickly during the early 20th century, particularly in the urban Northeast, Midwest, and California, while remaining relatively weak in the South. By 1936 had nearly 270,000 American members in more than 2,000 churches. By the late 1970s, Christian Science claimed about 475,000 members—mostly middle-class urbanites and suburbanites—and appealed to the spiritually curious through hundreds of "reading rooms" in the nation's malls and shopping districts.

The success of Christian Science encouraged the development of other, similar healing movements and organizations, usually urban in orientation and founded by people critical of Eddy's perceived autocracy. In Boston, Eddy critic Julius A. Dresser (1838–93) established the Church of the Higher Life in 1882. And in Chicago Christian Science apostate Emma Curtis Hopkins (1849–1925) organized followers in cities nationwide and established the Christian Science Theological Seminary in 1888. Her students in turn founded such movements as Divine Science, based in Denver, and Religious Science, based in Los Angeles. More successful than any of these was the Unity School of Christianity, established in Kansas City, Missouri, in 1889 and thereafter expanding into a national communications empire encompassing hundreds of local centers. In the 1890s, many of the various "mind cure" movements began to coalesce under the name "New Thought" and to form organizations—such as the National New Thought Alliance (1906)—to coordinate and facilitate activities nationwide. New Thought groups spread along roughly the same geographic and demographic lines as did Christian Science, and have maintained roughly the same regional distribution.

Despite small membership and distinct regional appeals, metaphysical movements remain viable alternatives and supplements to more conventional religiosity. They have also been highly influential, their success prompting many mainline Christian denominations to promote personal healing and their ideas figuring prominently in current New Age spirituality as Americans have continued to seek spiritual wholeness.

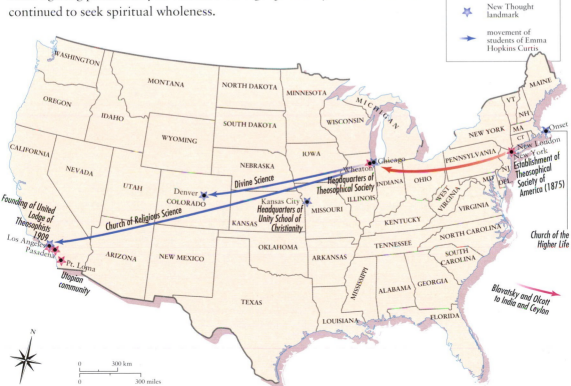

Metaphysical religions

Theosophy

⬥ Theosophy landmark

→ Theosophist emigration

→ relocation

New Thought

⬥ New Thought landmark

→ movement of students of Emma Hopkins Curtis

Communitarian Aspirations

Many Americans of the Northeast and Midwest founded religiously inspired communal societies as alternatives to 19th-century commercialization, capitalist competition, industrialization, and urbanization.

The longest-lived and perhaps best known is that of the Shakers (United Society of Believers in Christ's Second Coming), a group that originated in 18th-century England but flowered most fully in antebellum America. The movement was founded by Quaker Ann Lee (1736–84), who believed that sexual intercourse was the original sin, that she represented a second, female incarnation of God, and that she was to inaugurate the millennium by restoring the celibacy and sexual equality of Eden. Migrating to New York in 1774 to escape harassment in England, Lee and eight followers founded Watervliet, near Albany, in 1776 and then used revivalism to spread their message in New York and New England. Baptist converts founded a community at New Lebanon, New York in 1785, and within a decade eleven other communities appeared in New York, Massachusetts, Connecticut, New Hampshire, and Maine. Shakerism also moved westward, four more communities emerging in Ohio and Kentucky between 1805 and 1809 amid the Second Great Awakening. By the 1840s, when the movement peaked, there were about 6,000 Shakers in nineteen communities, all rural and agrarian, and all prospering under a strong ethic of work, spiritual discipline, and efficiency. But celibacy hampered their growth as accelerating urbanization and industrialization during the late 19th century deprived them of converts and threatened their isolation. Most disappeared by 1900, and today only the Maine community of Sabbathday Lake remains, a living but endangered testament to America's 19th-century search for spiritual meaning.

Also flowering in the New England–New York region was the movement founded by Vermonter John Humphrey Noyes (1811–86). Converted during an 1831 revival, he became convinced that Christ had returned to inaugurate the millennium in 70 CE and that sinless spiritual and social perfection was therefore possible. He gathered his followers into a community at Putney, Vermont, in 1836 to implement his doctrines, introducing "Bible communism" or common ownership of property in 1844 and then, in 1846, "complex marriage," in which sexual partners were shared in Christian love and children were raised communally. In 1848, local hostility drove the community, now several dozen strong, westward to Oneida, in New York's burned-over district. There, prospering through the manufacture of steel traps, the community endured for about three decades. It grew through conversion and procreation to about 205 members by 1851, and established six satellite communities between 1849 and 1851 in New York, New Jersey, Connecticut, and Vermont. Of these, all but that at Wallingford, Connecticut (1851), which manufactured silverware, proved short-lived. Eventually the combined membership of Oneida and Wallingford reached 306. But by 1881 economic success, secularization, internal dissension, resistance to Noyes's control, and external hostility destroyed the community.

The continuing communal inclinations of German pietist groups produced other long-lived—and in these cases ethnically defined—communitarian ventures. In 1804, George Rapp (1757–1847) and about 600 followers left Germany and its Lutheran church to establish Harmony in western Pennsylvania. Devoted to communal property ownership, rigid spiritual discipline, and (after 1807) celibacy, the community prospered. It moved west to Indiana in 1814, establishing the equally successful New Harmony colony on the Wabash River, and then returned to the Pittsburgh area to found Economy in eastern Ohio. An 1832 rebellion against Rapp diminished membership from 800 to about 500, and Rapp's death began a decline that ended with the community's 1905 dissolution, a full century after its inception.

Also successful was the Amana colony—or Community of True Inspiration—which had similar pietist origins. About 800 Inspirationists formed a community in the German Rhineland before migrating to the burned-over district in 1843 and founding Ebenezer near Buffalo. There the colony grew to six villages (including two nearby in Canada). In 1854, encroaching urbanization and desire for new land drove the colony westward to Iowa, where they established Amana, an isolated group of seven settlements on the Iowa River. There they enacted communal property arrangements and expanded to 1,800 members. Supported by a successful woolens industry, Amana prospered for several decades, but expanding westward settlement triggered decline in the late 19th century. It became a corporation in 1932, but its members founded the Amana Church Society, which numbered more than 500 in 1995.

By the late 19th century, intensifying transformation in the East and settlement in the Midwest had pushed most communitarian experimentation to the West, particularly New Mexico and California. Its persistence in the 20th century, particularly in the 1960s and 1970s, suggests the continuing spiritual hopes and anxieties of American life.

Communitarism

Shaker
→ expansion
● village, 1827

Oneida
→ expansion
● Oneida or associated community

Amana
→ expansion
● colony

Rappites
→ expansion
● colony

MAINE

Cambridge 1851
Sabbathday Lake
NH

NEW YORK   VT
Enfield   Alfred
Putney   Canterbury
1836   Shirley
Sodus Bay   Oneida   Harvard
Manlius   1848   Hancock
1851   Watervliet
Ebenezer   1851   Tyringham   MASS.
1843
New   Enfield
Lebanon   R.I.
North   Wallingford
Union   Harmony   1851
1804   PENNSYLVANIA
Newark
Economy   1825   1851   New York
OHIO   Brooklyn
1849
Shakers from Manchester, England

IOWA
Amana
1854
INDIANA
ILLINOIS
West   Watervliet
Union   Union Village
Whitewater
New Harmony
1815
Pleasant Hill
KENTUCKY   VIRGINIA
South Union

NEW JERSEY
Inspirationits from Rhineland, Germany
Rappites from Württenberg, Germany
MARYLAND
DEL.

N

0   100 km
0   100 miles

White Oak, Georgia
Narcoossee, Florida

Mormonism

Mormonism was perhaps the most successful new American religious movement of the 19th century, a small and persecuted sect that became a massive global church. Its early westward migrations were a singular religious expression of the larger contemporary story of American geographic expansion.

Mormonism emerged in New York's burned-over district, when Joseph Smith Jr. (1805–1844) of Palmyra, confused by revivalism and denominational competition in the area, experienced a series of religious visions. In them, the angels Mormon and Moroni revealed to him the existence of golden plates buried in nearby Manchester and containing a scriptural account of ancient America. According to the account—which Smith translated and published as the *Book of Mormon* (1830)—ancient Hebrews had migrated to America, been visited by Jesus, and fallen into infighting in which the Lamanites, ancestors of the Indians, exterminated the Nephites, leaving only Mormon and Moroni to record the events. Smith's uniquely "American" vision gave the nation a biblical past and promised to restore early Christianity there.

Smith and five followers formed a "Church of Jesus Christ" in Fayette, New York, in 1830, soon adding "of Latter-Day Saints" in anticipation of

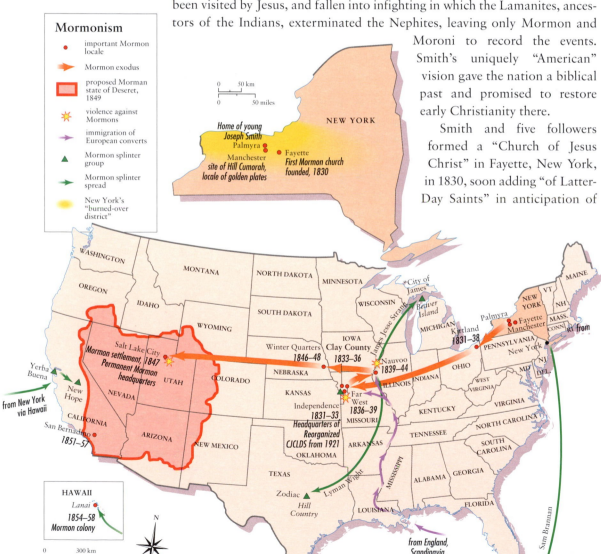

Mormonism

- important Mormon locale
- Mormon exodus
- proposed Morman state of Deseret, 1849
- violence against Mormons
- immigration of European converts
- Mormon splinter group
- Mormon splinter spread
- New York's "burned-over district"

0   50 km
0   50 miles

NEW YORK

Home of young Joseph Smith
Palmyra
Manchester
site of Hill Cumorah, locale of golden plates

Fayette
First Mormon church founded, 1830

WASHINGTON
MONTANA
NORTH DAKOTA
MINNESOTA
OREGON
IDAHO
SOUTH DAKOTA
WISCONSIN
City of James
Beaver Island
MICHIGAN
MAINE
NEW YORK
VT
NH
MASS.
CONN.
rd from
Palmyra
Fayette
Manchester

Salt Lake City
Mormon settlement, 1847
Permanent Mormon headquarters
UTAH
WYOMING
Winter Quarters
1846–48
IOWA
Clay County
1833–36
James Jesse Strang
Kirtland
1831–38
PENNSYLVANIA
New York
NJ
DEL.
MD
Yerba Buena
New Hope
from New York via Hawaii
NEVADA
COLORADO
NEBRASKA
Nauvoo
1839–44
Far West
1836–39
ILLINOIS
INDIANA
OHIO
WEST VIRGINIA
KANSAS
Independence
1831–33
Headquarters of Reorganized CJCLDS from 1921
MISSOURI
KENTUCKY
VIRGINIA
San Bernardino
1851–57
CALIFORNIA
ARIZONA
NEW MEXICO
OKLAHOMA
ARKANSAS
TENNESSEE
NORTH CAROLINA
SOUTH CAROLINA
TEXAS
Zodiac
Hill Country
Lyman Wight
Mississippi
LOUISIANA
ALABAMA
GEORGIA
FLORIDA
Sam Brannan

HAWAII
Lanai
1854–58
Mormon colony

0   300 km
0   300 miles

N

from England, Scandinavia, and Germany

to California via Hawaii

Christ's imminent Second Coming. It quickly expanded to several hundred, who regarded Smith as a prophet. Harassed in New York, Smith called for a "gathering" into a new Zion—making religious migration a central aspect of early Mormon experience—and in 1831 began Mormonism's series of westward treks. The group moved to Kirtland, Ohio, where they instituted a communal economy, dedicated a temple in 1836, arranged male church members into "Aaronic" and "Melchezedik" priesthoods based on ancient Hebrew models, attracted converts from among Campbellites and other restorationists, and began organizing missionary excursions to northwestern Europe.

Another group gathered in western Missouri after Smith announced that the biblical Eden lay there, and the Ohio group joined them after Kirtland's economy collapsed during the Panic of 1837. In Missouri, the Mormons, their numbers augmented by the immigration of European converts, dominated Caldwell, Daviess, Carroll, and Ray counties politically and economically. Religious differences and Mormon political power provoked area non-Mormons, resulting in a "Mormon War" in 1838 that drove perhaps 15,000 Mormons to Commerce, Illinois, in 1839. There they established the theocratic community of Nauvoo and built a new temple. At Nauvoo, Smith elaborated a systematic theology—including ongoing revelation, a corporeal and once-human god, and the development of human beings into gods—and developed such temple rituals as vicarious baptism of the dead. He also introduced "plural marriage," or polygamy. Religious, political, and economic tensions again arose between Mormons and their neighbors, culminating in Smith's

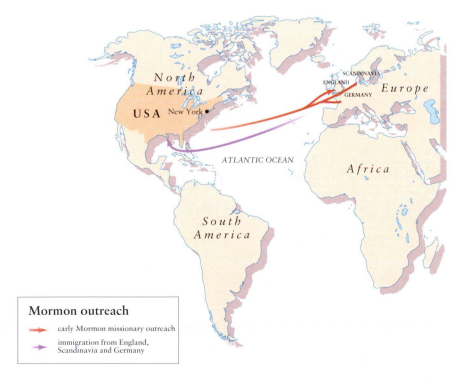

Mormon outreach

→ early Mormon missionary outreach

→ immigration from England,
   Scandinavia and Germany

This illustration depicts the persecution of early Mormons. Such hostility drove Mormons on a series of westward treks, eventually to Utah.

murder in 1844. By this time Nauvoo's population had grown to about 40,000.

Smith's death splintered the movement. His widow, Emma, and others rejected polygamy and the temple rituals, formed independent congregations across the Midwest, held an organizing conference in Wisconsin in 1853, and in 1860 formed the Reorganized Church of Jesus Christ of Latter Day Saints under Joseph Smith III. James Jesse Strang (1813–56) founded the theocratic "City of James" on Beaver Island in Lake Michigan in 1847 and led it until his murder in 1856. (A small remnant of his church still exists in Wisconsin.) Another group followed Lyman Wight to the Texas hill country, establishing the short-lived polygamous and communal colony of Zodiac in Burnet County. A contingent under Sam Brannan (1819–89) sailed to San Francisco and founded another short-lived colony, New Hope, in California's San Joaquin Valley.

About three-quarters of Smith's followers followed Brigham Young (1801–77) westward across the Plains to the Great Salt Lake Basin in a move they likened to the Hebrew exodus. They arrived in 1847 seeking to preserve Mormonism as Smith had developed it at Nauvoo. Envisioning a New Zion modeled on ancient Israel and a Mormon empire in the West, Young established the theocratic state of Deseret in 1849, constructed a massive irrigation system,

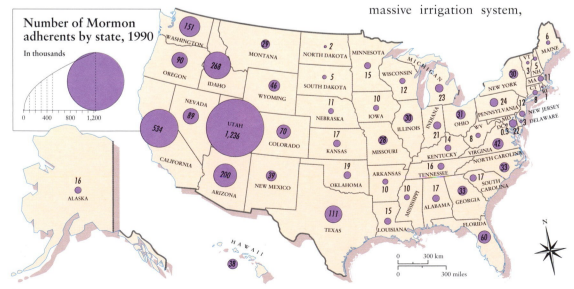

Number of Mormon adherents by state, 1990

In thousands

0   400   800   1,200

erected railroad and telegraph lines, oversaw Mormon expansion northward into Idaho and southward into Arizona, and attempted to set up colonies at San Bernardino (to facilitate immigration by way of San Diego) and on the Hawaiian island of Lanai. A regional religious counterculture developed, characterized by polygamy, a cooperative economy, a separate political party, and, some scholars argue, a distinct ethnic identity.

Fueled economically by transcontinental gold-rush migrations and numerically by an influx of converts from England, Germany, and Scandinavia, the region contained ninety communities by the late 1850s. By 1870 it was home to 86,000 people—perhaps 95 percent of them Mormon—and 160 of the nation's 189 Mormon churches. But tensions mounted between Mormons and federal authorities, especially after Young publicly announced the doctrine of plural marriage in 1852, and a "Utah War" ensued in 1857. The Utah territory, established in 1850 by a federal government mistrustful of Deseret, became a state in 1896 only after intensifying public and federal pressure against polygamy moved the Mormon church to abandon the practice in 1890.

Some disapproving Mormons formed underground polygamist groups, some of which survive in Utah, the Southwest, and Mexico. But most of them increasingly conformed to the wider culture in the 20th century. Mormon distinctiveness persisted in such behaviors as tithing and abstaining from tobacco, coffee, and alcohol, and a discernible Mormon "culture region"—in which some counties contain only Mormon churches—endures in the intermontane West. But Mormons have abandoned economic communalism. They also jettisoned the doctrine of gathering in favor of geographic dispersion and, indeed, global missionary outreach. Salt Lake City remains Mormonism's spiritual center and home to church headquarters, but Mormon "stakes" (parishes) have spread worldwide. With 4.7 million adherents in the United States alone, Mormonism has been an American success story.

Mormons as a percent of all church adherents, 1990

- 90
- 40
- 15
- 7
- 3
- 0.7
- 0.1

African-American Churches

African-American churches emerged and expanded dramatically during the 19th century, first in the North and then in the South. These churches combined west African and evangelical Protestant elements in a crucible shaped by enslavement, discrimination, and poverty to produce unique religious forms.

Early slaves resisted Christianity as alien, and efforts by the Society for the Propagation of the Gospel to convert them faltered for lack of missionaries and an emphasis on doctrine. But African Americans proved receptive to the evangelical impulses of the mid-18th and 19th centuries, for its experientialism, egalitarianism, emphasis on emotionally expressive lay preaching, and ecstatic audience participation coincided with west African tradition and counteracted white discrimination. Baptists and Methodists in particular attracted blacks and encouraged them to preach, and by 1790 the Methodists reported that nearly a fifth of their 60,000 converts were "colored." Baptist numbers were probably higher. The Second Great Awakening accelerated this trend.

The First Colored Baptist Church, Savannah, Georgia, 1794. African Americans of the 19th century increasingly formed independent congregations and, eventually, denominations.

In Northeastern cities, where abolition after the American Revolution allowed significant religious autonomy, free black Methodists formed separate congregations and denominations in the late 18th and early 19th centuries. In Philadelphia, lay preacher and former slave Richard Allen (1760–1831) founded the Bethel African Methodist Episcopal Church in 1794, and in 1816 met with representatives of black congregations in Pennsylvania, New Jersey, Delaware, and Maryland to form the African Methodist Episcopal (AME) Church. Spreading through the mid-Atlantic and Midwestern states, it grew to more

than 20,000 members by 1860. In New York, black congregations joined in 1821 to form the rival African Methodist Episcopal Zion (AMEZ) Church, which remained smaller than the AME Church—its membership was about 5,000 by 1860—but was politically active and included many leading black abolitionists. Black Methodists meeting in Wilmington, Delaware, in 1815 formed a third denomination, the Union Church of Africans.

African Americans of other denominations formed separate institutions as well. Black Baptist congregations appeared in Boston, New York, and Philadelphia by 1809, and by the 1830s began combining into regional associations. In Philadelphia, black Episcopalians formed a congregation in 1794, and Presbyterians did likewise in 1807. All of these institutions promoted racial identity and were central to the social, political, economic, and cultural life of Northern, free, urban, black communities. Many actively promoted abolitionism and migration along the Underground Railroad.

Church formation was more problematic in the South until after the Civil War. Some slave owners permitted separate slave worship in local chapels, and a number of black congregations—mostly Baptist, with some Methodist and Presbyterian—developed in the late 18th and 19th centuries. Some urban Baptist churches became quite large: Gillfield, in Petersburg, Virginia, had 441 members in 1821, and Charleston's First African claimed more than 2,400 by 1830. But most African-American congregations were short-lived, and whites curtailed autonomous black gatherings after Christianity's implication in the Denmark Vesey (1822) and Nat Turner (1831) slave rebellions. Most Christian slaves attended integrated but white-dominated churches, most of which were Methodist since the denomination actively promoted plantation missions, and

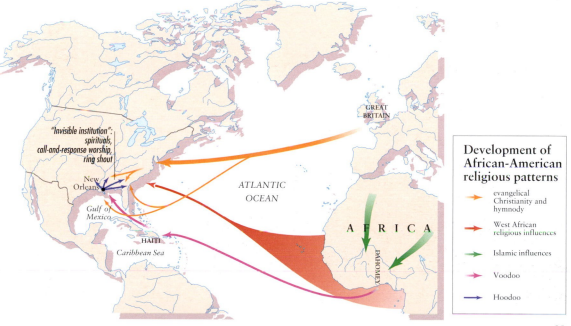

85

its silence on the slavery issue before 1844 (when the denomination split along sectional lines) made its preachers welcome on plantations. Many slaves also practiced a covert and distinctive form of worship—characterized by enthusiastic preaching, spirituals, and a call-and-response format reminiscent of west African practices—often called the "invisible institution."

Emancipation and Reconstruction sparked the growth of existing black denominations and the formation of new ones. During the Civil War, many blacks left the white Methodist Episcopal Church, South for the AME and AMEZ churches, which had moved into the South in the wake of Union Army advances. By war's end in 1865, the AME church had grown to more than 50,000 members and the AMEZ to more than 30,000; by 1896, those numbers had expanded to about 450,000 and 350,000, respectively. Other freed slaves resisted the Northern black churches and established indigenous Southern denominations, often by separating from white organizations. Colored Primitive Baptists and the African Union First Colored Methodist Protestant Church organized in 1866; in 1869, blacks formed the Reformed Zion Union Apostolic Church, and the Colored Cumberland Presbyterian Church split off from its white counterpart; the Colored (later Christian) Methodist Episcopal (CME) Church broke away from the Methodist Episcopal Church, South in 1870; the Colored Presbyterian Church from the mainline Presbyterian Church in

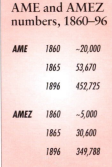

AME and AMEZ numbers, 1860–96		
AME	1860	~20,000
	1865	53,670
	1896	452,725
AMEZ	1860	~5,000
	1865	30,600
	1896	349,788

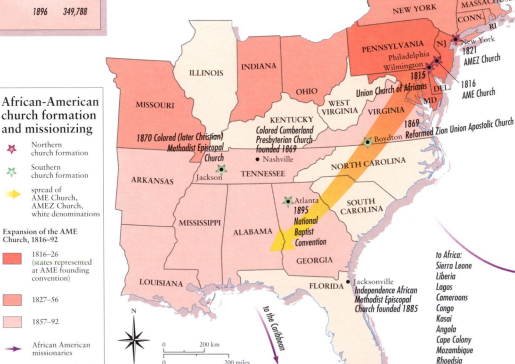

African-American church formation and missionizing

✶ Northern church formation

✶ Southern church formation

➜ spread of AME Church, AMEZ Church, white denominations

Expansion of the AME Church, 1816–92

■ 1816–26 (states represented at AME founding convention)

■ 1827–56

■ 1857–92

➜ African American missionaries

1874; in 1885, a group of Southern blacks left the Northern-dominated AME church to form the Independent African Methodist Episcopal Church. Finally, in 1895, black Baptist associations nationwide merged in Atlanta into the huge National Baptist Convention (NBC). Ministers in these churches often promoted racial consciousness, many participating actively in Reconstruction politics and some, like AME bishop Henry Turner (1834–1915), advocating migration to Africa. Black churches also sent missionaries to blacks in Africa and the West Indies. By 1990, four of nineteen AME districts were in Africa.

Not all African Americans of the 19th century embraced evangelical Protestantism. In Maryland and Louisiana, many slaves accepted their owners' Catholicism, and migrations from Maryland to Kentucky in the late 18th and early 19th centuries included many black Catholic slaves. French-speaking migrants to New Orleans and Baltimore from politically unstable Saint Domingue (Haiti) beginning in the 1790s further augmented those numbers (as has 20th-century Caribbean migration to New York and Florida). Other Afro-Caribbean migrants from Saint Domingue to New Orleans brought *voodoo*, which combined west African traditions of dance and spirit possession with ritual Catholic candles, altars, and prayers. The most direct African religious importation to America, it flourished in New Orleans by 1850, and its healing practices spread throughout the slave South as *hoodoo*. Still other blacks retained the Islam to which they had been exposed in Africa. But the mid-1990s figures—5 million in the AME, AMEZ, and CME churches, and 12 million in the descendants of the NBC—suggest the continuing dominance of evangelical Protestantism in African-American religion.

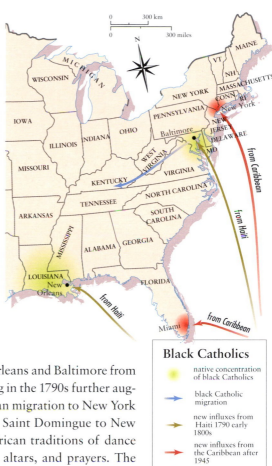

Black Catholics

- native concentration of black Catholics
- → black Catholic migration
- → new influxes from Haiti 1790 early 1800s
- → new influxes from the Caribbean after 1945
- new concentration of black Catholics

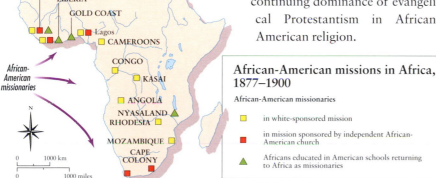

African-American missions in Africa, 1877–1900

African-American missionaries

- □ in white-sponsored mission
- ■ in mission sponsored by independent African-American church
- ▲ Africans educated in American schools returning to Africa as missionaries

PART V: WORLD RELIGIONS AND GROWING PLURALISM, 1850–PRESENT

The years around 1850 represented a watershed in American religious history, for they marked the onset of a series of waves of immigration from Asia, Africa, Latin America, Europe, and the Middle East that transformed a largely Protestant landscape into a new and far more pluralistic one that, dotted with new churches, synagogues, temples, and mosques, encompassed nearly the entire kaleidoscopic array of the world's religions.

The first wave began in the late 1840s and brought millions of Irish Catholics to the urban Northeast. Then, from 1880 to 1920, American industrial cities and mining towns from the East Coast to the Great Lakes were peopled by a "new" immigration far larger and more varied than the "old" immigration patterns that had brought white westward-moving Christians—mostly Protestant Christians—from northern and western Europe. Now arriving from eastern and southern Europe were Jews, Catholics, and Eastern Orthodox. From there and from the Near and Middle East came, initially in smaller numbers, Muslims. Asian immigrants, meanwhile, streamed eastward across the Pacific Ocean to the West Coast, bringing Buddhism, Hinduism, Sikhism, and other Asian religions to the cities and rural interior. Somewhat later, in the early 20th century, agricultural and urban expansion in the West and Southwest attracted northward-moving Mexican Catholics. Restrictive legislation in the 1920s reduced most of these streams to a trickle, but 1965 revisions, coupled with ongoing economic expansion in the United States and political turmoil elsewhere in the world, have sparked immigration from all directions, particularly from southern and southeastern Asia, Latin America, the Caribbean, and the Middle East. Religiously as well as demographically and physically, the United States became vastly different from what it had been in 1850.

Arriving to work in the nation's expanding systems of large-scale industrial production and agricultural production, immigrants often formed ethnic communities, sometimes in rural areas but far more often, and in much greater numbers, in the nation's cities, particularly those of the Northeast, Midwest, and West Coast. Cities became places of intercultural contact and conflict as immigrants living among peoples of varying ethnicities and nationalities and in a new American setting moved to defend or to transform their distinct religious traditions and cultures. Exacerbating these religiocultural tensions were social ones resulting from differences—often a function of order of arrival—in level of cultural assimilation, status, affluence, and power, as well as generational ones, with immigrants' children often proving more willing and able to adapt than their parents. Such ethnic tensions often inhibited unity within religious traditions, generating multiple and competing ethnically based institutions which became foci of ethnic group loyalty and centers of social, cultural, and educational life. On the other hand, religious institutions as readily fostered interethnic unity as ethnic exclusiveness.

America's transformation from a largely "Judeo-Christian" culture to a far more multiethnic and multireligious one was heralded, symbolized, and promoted by the World's Parliament of Religions, held in Chicago in 1893. Held in conjunction with the Columbian Exposition that celebrated the 400th anniversary of the European colonization of the Americas, this gathering of representatives of many of the world's religions (including twelve Buddhists, eight Hindus, two Muslims, three Zoroastrians, two Shintoists, one Daoist, and one Jain) was organized by Protestants eager to promote Christianity. But the conference in fact spearheaded the entry of non-Western religions into American life by giving voice to diverse traditions and serving as a springboard for lecture tours and institution formation. The many voices at the parliament announced the highly pluralistic American religious culture aborning on the eve of the 20th century.

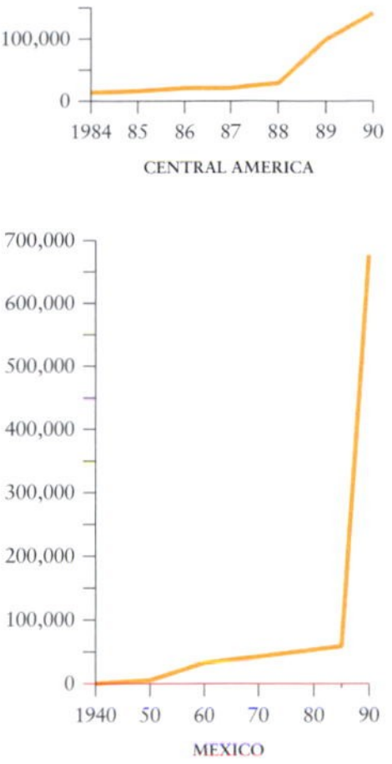

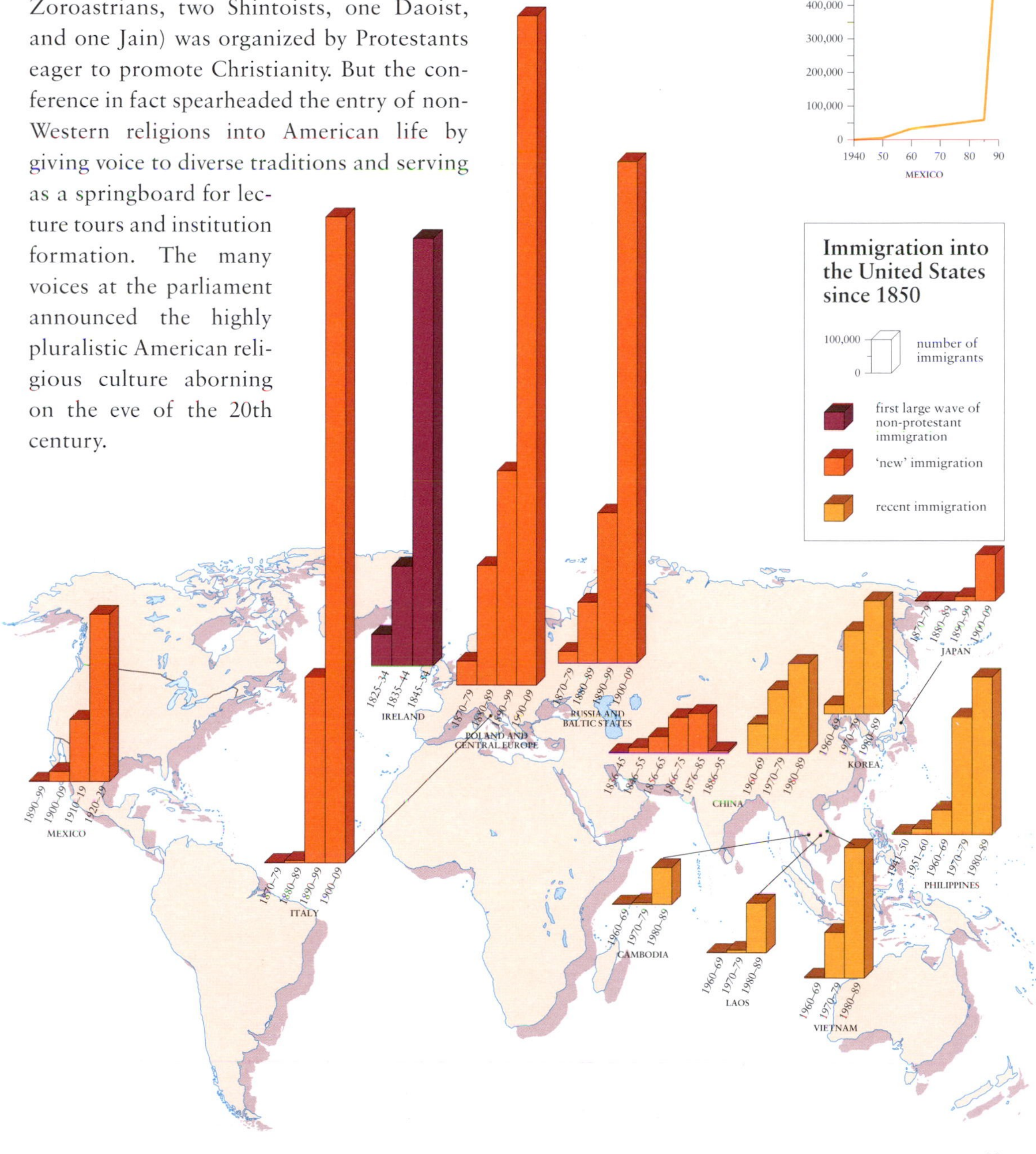

Immigration into the United States since 1850

100,000 — number of immigrants
0

first large wave of non-protestant immigration

'new' immigration

recent immigration

CENTRAL AMERICA

MEXICO

MEXICO

ITALY

IRELAND

POLAND AND CENTRAL EUROPE

RUSSIA AND BALTIC STATES

CHINA

KOREA

JAPAN

PHILIPPINES

CAMBODIA

LAOS

VIETNAM

The Growth of American Catholicism

John Ireland, Archbishop of St. Paul (1875–1918), was an advocate of Americanization and one of the nation's foremost Roman Catholic leaders.

Catholicism in Europe was under papal control, officially established in several countries, and, because tied to diverse national cultures, multiform. In the United States it grew (but at times suffered attrition) as the American church tried to adapt to Protestant dominance, republicanism, a secularizing culture, and expanding religious and ethnic pluralism.

At the start of the 19th century, the church's American membership was only about 50,000, and its hierarchy, appointed by Rome and dominated by English and French Americans, was resisted on political grounds by democratically elected lay trustees of church property and on ethnic ones by minority Irish and German Catholics. Trustee conflicts erupted in many major cities, and Philadelphia Germans formed an independent church in 1787. The church resolved trustee problems by transferring church property to bishops, but ethnic tensions intensified, expanded, and assumed regional variation as the church and nation grew. Louisiana's French- and Spanish-speaking Catholics resisted their new American authorities after the Louisiana Purchase (1803), while the French bishop appointed to New Mexico after it became an American possession in 1848 sought unsuccessfully to eradicate the Spanish-Mexican-Indian cultural blend of its Native American Catholics. Tensions similar to those in New Mexico simmered in formerly Mexican California.

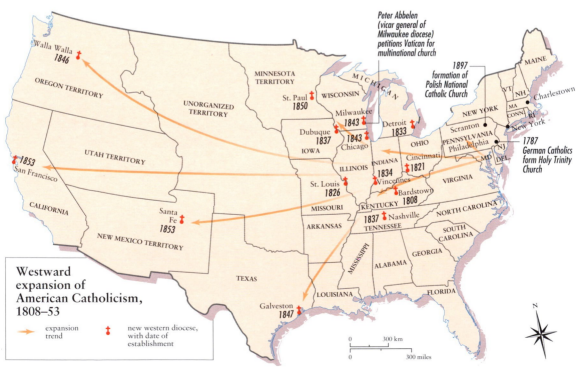

The phenomenal growth and increasing ethnic diversity of 19th-century American Catholicism were driven above all by massive waves of European immigration that lifted its numbers past 3 million by 1860—making it the nation's largest denomination—and past 12 million by 1900. The first wave brought Irish victims of the Potato Famine of the late 1840s. About 1.5 million reached America between 1845 and 1860 and another 1.5 million between 1870 and 1900. Settling in Northeastern cities—especially Boston, New York, and Philadelphia—they were confined by poverty and discrimination to slums and unskilled industrial jobs. But many sought opportunity and status in the priesthood, and Irish Catholics soon dominated the church hierarchy. German Catholics also arrived in the 19th century—several hundred thousand by 1850 and more than a million more by 1900—settling a Midwestern "German Triangle" defined by Cincinnati, Milwaukee, and St. Louis as well as the eastern Ozarks and the central Texas hill country. They formed tight ethnic communities and resisted the Irish American hierarchy.

Meanwhile, the church expanded with the nation to the Pacific. In 1800 the only diocese was Baltimore, with other Northeastern cities following soon after. But Catholic migration from Maryland to Kentucky and western Pennsylvania prompted the formation of the Bardstown (Kentucky) diocese in 1808. As the church reached out to French Catholics in the Mississippi Valley and Great Lakes areas, to Germans in Texas and the Midwest, to Catholic Indians in the Southwest, and to white Americans moving to the Pacific region, it founded dioceses in Cincinnati (1821), St. Louis (1826), Detroit (1833), Vincennes (1834), Dubuque (1837), Nashville

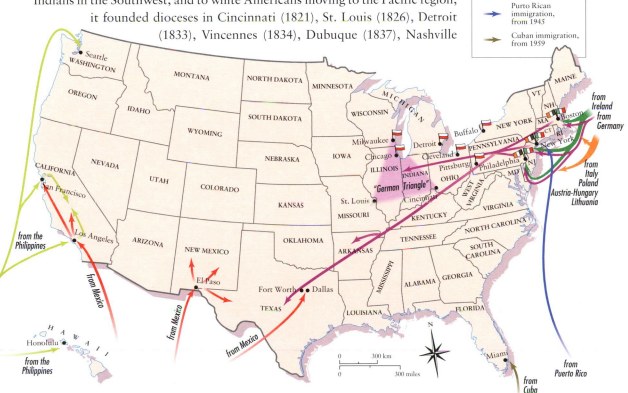

Catholic immigration patterns

- → Irish immigration, 1820s and after
- → German immigration, 1815 and after
- → "new" immigration, 1880–1915
- 🚩 city of heavy Polish settlement
- 🚩 city of heavy Italian settlement
- 🚩 city of heavy Irish settlement
- → Mexican immigration, from 1895
- → Filipino immigration, from 1898
- → Puerto Rican immigration, from 1945
- → Cuban immigration, from 1959

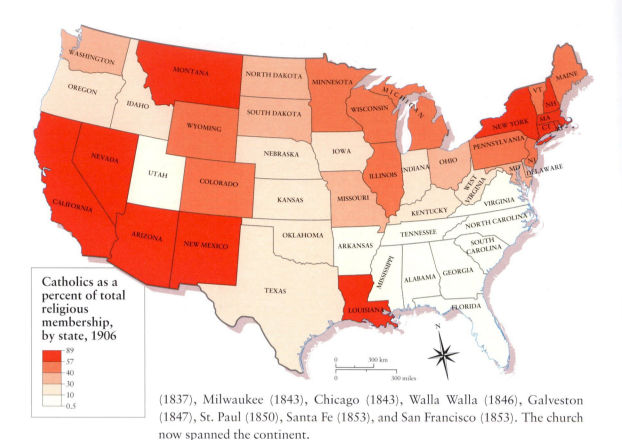

Catholics as a percent of total religious membership, by state, 1906

- 89
- 57
- 40
- 30
- 10
- 0.5

(1837), Milwaukee (1843), Chicago (1843), Walla Walla (1846), Galveston (1847), St. Paul (1850), Santa Fe (1853), and San Francisco (1853). The church now spanned the continent.

After 1880, a "new" immigration brought Catholics from southern, eastern, and central Europe to the agricultural areas of the Great Plains and, in far greater numbers, the industrial cities of the Northeast and Midwest. About 3.3 million southern Italians arrived by 1920, forming ethnic enclaves in Boston, Harlem, and Philadelphia, mistrusting the Irish-American hierarchy, and practicing a family-centered folk Catholicism. Polish Catholic immigrants—some 3 million by 1920—formed "Polonias" in such Great Lakes cities as Chicago, Detroit, Milwaukee, Cleveland, and Buffalo. Protective of their culture, they unsuccessfully sought greater representation in the hierarchy and successfully formed enduring Polish dioceses. Some broke away to form the Polish National Catholic Church in Scranton, Pennsylvania, in 1897. Other Catholics arrived from Austro-Hungary, Lithuania, and other European countries. American church leaders responded to the growing diversity by encouraging Americanization—including English-language parochial instruction, attendance at public schools, and acceptance of religious pluralism—while disapproving German leaders in the Midwest unsuccessfully petitioned Rome for a multinational and multilingual American church with ethnically rather than geographically defined dioceses.

Despite continuing ethnic tensions and a papal condemnation of perceived "Americanization," a curbing of European immigration in the 1920s and the pope's 1908 declaration that the United States was no longer a mission field heralded the American church's growing consolidation and underscored its changing relationship with Rome. After World War II, Catholics became more fully integrated into American life, obtaining white-collar jobs, leaving their old neighborhoods, and joining the exodus to the suburbs and the Sunbelt. Rome remained—and remains—anxious about liberalizing trends in American Catholicism.

Twentieth-century migration and immigration posed new challenges of ethnic diversity. After 1890, Mexicans seeking agricultural employment moved northward with their folk Catholicism into Texas, the Southwest, and California, creating anew a Hispanic Catholic region in the United States. After the Spanish-American War of 1898, Filipinos joined a growing eastward-moving trans-Pacific Asian migration to Hawaii (annexed by the United States in 1898), the West Coast, and eventually the East. Other new pockets of Hispanic Catholicism developed after World War II, when Puerto Ricans increasingly settled in New York City and thousands of middle-class Cubans fleeing the 1959 revolution brought their brand of Catholicism to the Miami area. Finally, Central Americans fleeing political and economic turmoil entered the United States during the 1970s and 1980s. By 1989, about 20 percent of Hispanic Catholics, alienated by the American hierarchy, had converted to evangelical and Pentecostal Protestantism—in cities, attending storefront churches. Others sought greater power within the church, as exemplified by the founding of the National Catholic Council for Hispanic Ministry in 1990. Most Latinos still consider themselves Catholic, but the percentage dropped from 90 percent in the late 1960s to about 70 percent in the 1990s.

American Catholicism continues to grapple with challenges of Americanization and ethnic diversity. Encompassing one-quarter of the nation's population, however, its established place in American life is clear.

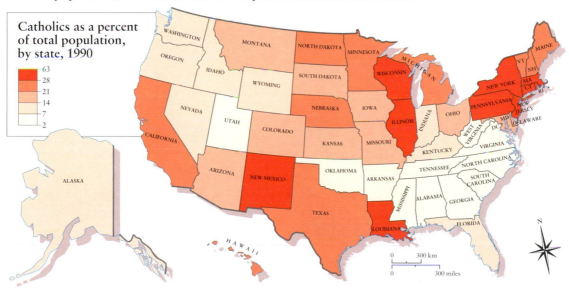

Catholics as a percent of total population, by state, 1990

63
28
21
14
7
2

The Development of American Judaism

Colonial American Jews were largely Sephardic, prosperous, and urban, living in the Atlantic seaports. But 19th-century immigration produced wider geographic dispersion, increasing ethnic diversity, and tensions over Americanization.

Between 1830 and 1860, German and Austro-Hungarian Ashkenazic immigration raised America's Jewish population from 6,000 to 150,000. Most of the immigrants were less prosperous and became itinerant peddlers on the expanding frontier; others succeeded as dry goods merchants in the small towns and larger cities, particularly in the Northeast and the Midwestern "German Triangle." Migrants from the same region in Europe tended to settle together in America: Bavarians in Cincinnati and Cleveland, southern Germans in Atlanta, Austro-Hungarians in Milwaukee. Jewish communities existed nationwide by 1860, with particularly substantial ones in New York and Cincinnati.

With the German influx came Reform Judaism, which emphasized assimilation, ethics, and vernacular worship over traditional Hebrew-language ritual and ethnic distinctiveness. Many existing congregations embraced Reform, and new Reform synagogues proliferated: Har Sinai in Baltimore (1842), Emanu-El in New York (1845), and Sinai in Chicago (1858). Leading the Reform thrust was Bohemian immigrant rabbi Isaac Mayer Wise (1819–1900), who arrived in 1846, established a base at Cincinnati's Bene Yeshurun, gathered Reform congregations into the Union of American Hebrew Congregations (1873), and founded Hebrew Union College (1875), the nation's first permanent rabbinical school. In 1889, Reform rabbis meeting in Detroit completed the organization of American Reform Judaism by forming the Central Conference of American Rabbis (CCAR). By 1880, most of America's 250,000 Jews and 270 synagogues were Reform and of Germanic background.

Those opposing the extent of Americanization often formed separate institutions. Ethnic difference sometimes bolstered conservative impulses, as when traditionalist Polish and Russian Jews in New York, resistant to German leadership, founded Shaarey Zedek (1839) and Beth Hamedrash (1852), respectively. As Reform became institutionalized, so too did a Conservative "middle way" between Americanization and tradition, first in the founding of the Jewish Theological Seminary

Plum Street Synagogue, Cincinnati. Jewish immigration to Northeastern and Midwestern cities after the mid-19th century made Judaism a major American faith.

(JTS) in 1886 and later in the establishment of the United Synagogue of America (1913; now the United Synagogue of Conservative Judaism) and the Rabbinical Assembly of America (1919).

Jewish traditionalism was strengthened and ethnically expanded when the "new" immigration brought more than 2 million Eastern European Jews from Russia, Poland, Lithuania, Ukraine, and Romania to the nation's Northern industrial cities between 1880 and 1920. By 1927, they accounted for about 80 percent of American Jewry. They settled especially in New York's Lower East Side, home by 1892 to more than one-third of America's Jews. But while concerned to preserve tradition, the new arrivals were alienated from established Reform and Conservative Jewish communities by class, cultural, and linguistic differences. The immigrants formed ethnic enclaves and congregations, protected their vernacular Yiddish (a Germanic language written in Hebrew and with Hebrew, Russian, and Polish infusions), and formed an "Orthodox" denomination distinct from Reform and Conservatism, institutionalizing it in the Rabbi Isaac Elchanan Theological Seminary on the Lower East Side (1897), the Union of Orthodox Jewish Congregations in America (1898), and the Union of Orthodox Rabbis (1902).

American Judaism became even more ethnically and religiously diverse during the 20th century as the Russian Revolution of 1917 and the rise of Nazism in the 1930s and 1940s sparked an immigration of eastern European Hasidim, practitioners of a pietistic, mystically inclined, and ultratraditional variety of Judaism. They formed insulated communities, mostly in Brooklyn, where they adhered strictly to traditional ritual, Yiddish, and eastern European lifestyles. Some communities sought even greater isolation in upstate New

Judaism

→ German and Austro-Hungarian immigration, 1820–60 Reform Judaism

→ Eastern European (Russian, Lithuanian, Polish, Ukrainian, Rumanian) immigration, 1880–1924 Orthodox Judaism

→ Hasidic immigration from Poland and Central Europe, 1930s and 1940s

→ recent Jewish immigration from South Africa, South America, and Israel, 1960s and 1970s

→ American Jewish emigration to Israel, 1960s–

✳ early Sephardic/Ashkenazic tensions

★ early Ashkenazic congregations

Brooklyn
Hasidic communities
New York City
1880s–1950s
center of American Judaism

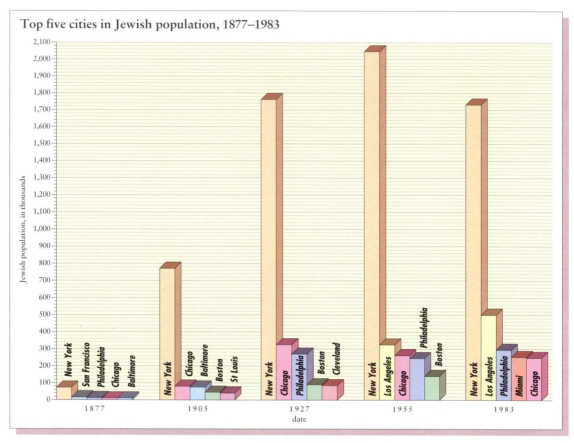

Top five cities in Jewish population, 1877–1983

York, while other groups, such as the Brooklyn-based Lubavitcher, have engaged in missionary outreach to young Jews. Today, about 80 percent of the world's approximately 250,000 Hasidim live in the United States, half of these in Brooklyn. The Hasidic presence is small but has invigorated American Orthodoxy and the Old World ties of American Judaism generally. Still more recently, in the 1960s and 1970s, Jewish immigrants have arrived from the Soviet Union, South Africa, South America, and Israel. In the 1980s, 5 to 10 percent of American Jews were recent immigrants. Ethnicity and immigration thus remain central themes of American Jewish experience.

Still, most American Jews became thoroughly integrated into American life. The children of Orthodox immigrants joined the suburban exodus of the 1950s, abandoned Orthodoxy, Yiddish, and the old neighborhoods in the pursuit of affluence, swelled Reform and Conservative ranks, and built new suburban synagogues. They also followed the broader post–World War II migration to the Sunbelt, producing major new communities in Los Angeles and Miami and modifying their traditional Northeastern and Midwestern concentration. Still, New York City's approximately 1.5 million Jews—and more if one includes the surrounding metropolitan area—remain America's largest concentration, and nearly half of the nation's Jews still live in the Northeast.

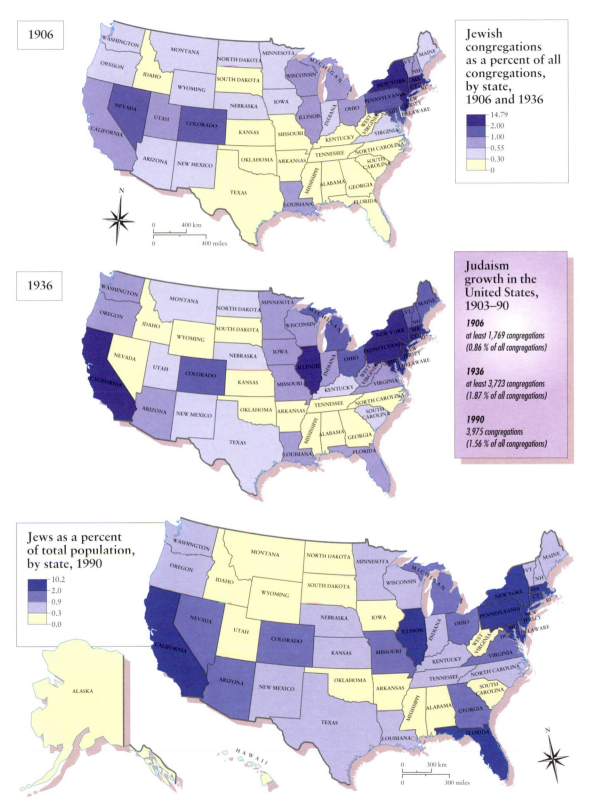

1906

Jewish
congregations
as a percent of all
congregations,
by state,
1906 and 1936

- 14.79
- 2.00
- 1.00
- 0.55
- 0.30
- 0

1936

**Judaism
growth in the
United States,
1903–90**

1906
at least 1,769 congregations
(0.86 % of all congregations)

1936
at least 3,723 congregations
(1.87 % of all congregations)

1990
3,975 congregations
(1.56 % of all congregations)

Jews as a percent
of total population,
by state, 1990

- 10.2
- 2.0
- 0.9
- 0.3
- 0.0

Eastern Orthodoxy in America

Eastern Orthodoxy is a sacramental and iconic form of Christianity that diverged from Roman Catholicism in late antiquity and was centered in Eastern Europe and the eastern Mediterranean basin. It became a major presence in America with the "new" immigration. During the decades after 1880, about a million Eastern Orthodox from Russia, Greece, Ukraine, Albania, Serbia, Romania, Bulgaria, and Syria and other countries moved through New York (which became their major population center) to the Pennsylvania coal fields, the industrial cities of the Midwest and Northeast, and, in smaller numbers, the West Coast. In the Old World a decentralized "family" of separate national churches, tied to varying languages, cultures, and political systems, Eastern Orthodox churches remained diverse in America. Their members formed tight ethnic communities, coexisted uneasily, and formed a kaleidoscopic array of bodies.

The Russians were the most significant early Orthodox presence, colonizing Alaska during the late 18th century and then, during the 19th, converting more than 10,000 natives (perhaps a sixth of Alaska's population) and establishing a diocese in Sitka. The Russian presence—though not the natives' Russian Orthodoxy—yielded to a growing American Protestant presence after the 1867 sale of Alaska to the United States. In 1872 the Russian Orthodox church transferred the diocese southward to San Francisco to serve the growing city's Russian, Greek, Serbian, and Syrian Orthodox. Orthodox immigration to the Northeast and Midwest after 1880 revitalized Russian Orthodoxy in America and shifted its focus eastward. Under Archbishop Tikhon Belavin (1865–1925), the Russian church established dominance over American Orthodoxy, the Diocese of the Aleutians and Alaska became the Diocese of the Aleutians and North America, the Church of St. Nicholas was erected in New York in 1901, and the diocese was

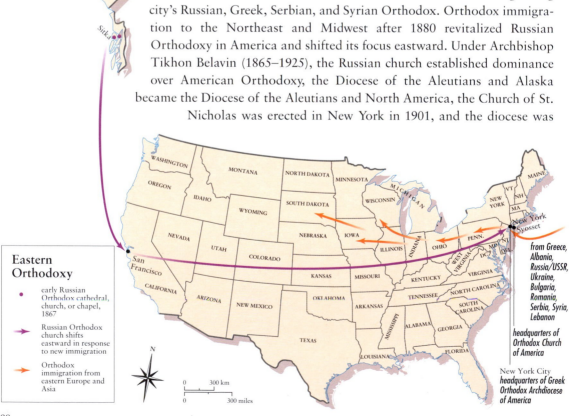

Eastern Orthodoxy

- early Russian Orthodox cathedral, church, or chapel, 1867

→ Russian Orthodox church shifts eastward in response to new immigration

→ Orthodox immigration from eastern Europe and Asia

from Greece, Albania, Russia/USSR, Ukraine, Bulgaria, Romania, Serbia, Syria, Lebanon

headquarters of Orthodox Church of America

New York City *headquarters of Greek Orthodox Archdiocese of America*

0   300 km

0   300 miles

The Russian Orthodox cathedral dedicated to St Michael, built in Sitka, Alaska in 1848, seen in this photograph taken around 1900.

moved to New York in 1905—making Orthodoxy the only Christian tradition in America whose center of gravity moved from west to east.

Seeking a "pan-Orthodox" American church under Russian jurisdiction and English liturgy, the Russian church expanded by 1916 to 100,000 members by attracting Syrians, Serbs, Bulgarians, and "Uniates" (eastern European Christians loyal to Rome but alienated from the American Catholic hierarchy after arriving from Russia and Ukraine) in addition to the Slavs and native Alaskans who remained its primary constituents. But the nationalist impulses of World War I and the 1917 rise of communism in Russia shattered this developing arrangement into separate ethnic churches resistant to Moscow. Romanians separated from the Russian church in 1918 and formed a church in 1921, followed by Serbs, Albanians, Syrians, Bulgarians, and Ukrainians. After World War II, these churches grew under renewed immigration and consolidated into such current bodies as the Antiochian (Syrian) Orthodox Christian Archdiocese of North America (250,000 members), the Bulgarian Eastern Orthodox Church (105,000), the Serbian Eastern Orthodox Church (50,000), and the Romanian Orthodox Episcopate of America (40,000). Other, smaller churches represented Albanians, Egyptians, Armenians, Ukrainians, former Uniates, and several other groups. In addition to spinning off these ethnically defined churches, the Russian church itself split into three separate organizations—all with American headquarters in or near New York City—over the question of allegiance to Moscow in the wake of the Russian Revolution. The largest of these maintained a tense connection with Russia until achieving independence in 1970 as the Orthodox Church of America (OCA). It has retained intellectual dominance over American Orthodoxy, become increasingly multiethnic, and renewed its ties to Alaska natives.

Greek Orthodox as a percent of religious membership, by state, 1936

1.53
0.60
0.40
0.15
0.03
0.00

The several hundred thousand Greek Orthodox who arrived from Greece, Asia Minor, and the Mediterranean islands between the 1890s and 1920s resisted Russian hegemony and formed separate parishes. The first, established in New York (1892) and Chicago (1893), were followed by 1921 by more than 160 others, mostly in New York, Massachusetts, Pennsylvania, Ohio, and Illinois. In 1922 these formed the Greek Archdiocese of North and South America, based in New York City. Beginning in the 1930s, the church attracted Uniates,

Greek Orthodox churches, by state, 1990

20
10
0

number

Albanians, Byelorussians and others. It became and remains the nation's largest Orthodox church. By 1995 its United States membership of nearly 2 million was sufficiently large to warrant the formation of a separate archdiocese.

Americanization remains an important issue for American Orthodox, as manifested on the one hand by continuing ethnic consciousness and retention by many churches of their traditional languages and liturgies, and on the other by Orthodox leaders' desire to be recognized as a major American faith.

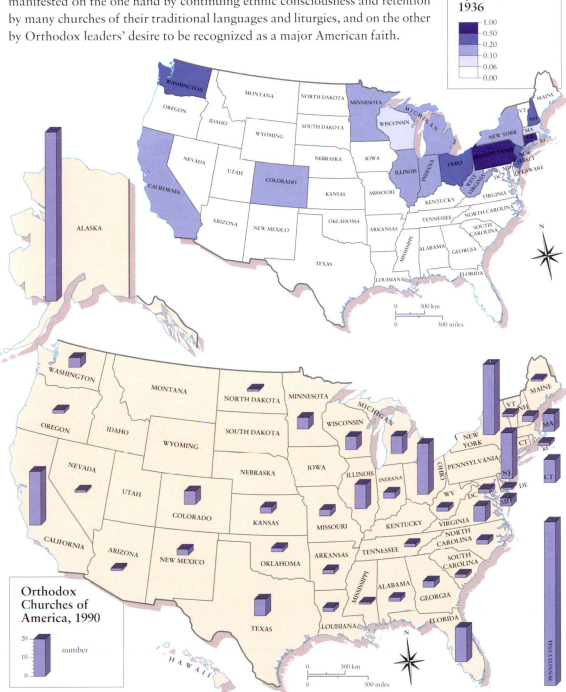

Russian Orthodox as a percent of religious membership, by state, 1936

- 1.00
- 0.50
- 0.20
- 0.10
- 0.06
- 0.00

Orthodox Churches of America, 1990

- 20
- 10
- 0

number

Islam in America

The tremendous growth of Islam in 20th-century America—in which immigration, propagation, and conversions have made it the nation's third-largest (perhaps second-largest) religion—is a powerful indicator of the expansion of American religion beyond Judeo-Christian tradition. But like Christianity and Judaism, it is a monotheistic, scriptural faith. Teaching submission to God, or Allah, it requires daily prayer facing its birthplace in Mecca, Saudi Arabia, almsgiving, a month of fasting each year, and pilgrimage to Mecca.

Having spread across the Near and Middle East, eastward to India and the East Indies, westward to Spain, Portugal, and northern and western Africa, southward into east Africa, and northward into southeastern Europe, Islam came to North America in the 16th and 17th centuries with Spanish colonizers and the African slave trade. (Fifteen to 20 percent of African-American slaves were Muslim by some estimates.) Some white Americans began to show interest in Islam in the late 19th century, and Alexander Russell Webb (1846–1916), U.S. consul to the Philippines, founded a short-lived mosque (Muslim place of worship) in New York after converting in Manila in 1888.

Late 19th and early 20th centuries

area of Islam

migration

The new immigration produced the first significant and enduring American Muslim communities. Relatively small numbers arrived in the late 19th century—mostly from Syria, Jordan, (what is now) Lebanon, Turkey, the Balkans, and Poland—and settled in the industrial cities of the Northeast and Midwest. New York and Chicago became important population centers for them, but attraction to the automobile industry produced noteworthy communities in Michigan, including Detroit and Dearborn. Other significant communities appeared in Cedar Rapids, Iowa, and—for eastern European Muslims—Buffalo, New York. In the early 20th century, Muslims from India and Pakistan established enduring communities in California's agricultural regions. But prior to World War II American Muslims were largely of Arab origin and numbered only several thousand.

A much larger and more diverse influx occurred after World War Two, particularly after immigration laws were liberalized in 1965. Syrian and Lebanese immigrants were now joined by larger numbers of Indians and Pakistanis seeking economic opportunity, Albanians and Yugoslavs fleeing communism, Egyptians and Iranians fleeing political oppression, and Palestinians fleeing the new state of Israel. Students too arrived in large numbers from across North Africa, the Middle East, and south and Southeast Asia. Arabs remained the largest element in American Islam, but by the 1980s immigration had made south Asians a particularly substantial presence and, in combination with

African-American conversions to Islam, swelled the number of mosques from about twenty in the early 1970s to more than 1,000 by the 1990s.

With expansion came national organization, growing interethnic unity, and a degree of Americanization. American Muslims founded the Federation of Islamic Associations in 1954, followed in 1981 by the Islamic Society of North America. And while traditional differences persist between Islam's Sunni and Shi'ite sects, the American setting has minimized them. Muslim practice, too, has changed, with Sundays becoming increasingly important for community gatherings and the religious education of the young. Worship in Arabic remains mandatory and widespread, but sermons and informal prayer in English have helped promote community in the growing number of multiethnic mosques. Such organizations as the American Muslim Council and the Council of American Islamic Relations have promoted interaction between African-American and ethnic Arab Muslims.

Despite these changes, American Islam's early geographic pattern remains. Immigrant Muslims and their descendants remain most heavily concentrated in the cities of the Northeast and Midwest and, outside those regions, in such urban areas as Houston, Los Angeles, and San Francisco. Other concentrated communities have formed in places climatically similar to countries of origin, as with Iranians and Arabs in Florida, Texas, Arizona, and southern California, or geographically convenient, as with Muslims from south Asia and the Pacific Basin in Honolulu, San Francisco, and Seattle.

Encompassing perhaps 8 million Americans and present in most sizable American towns, Islam has become a major American faith.

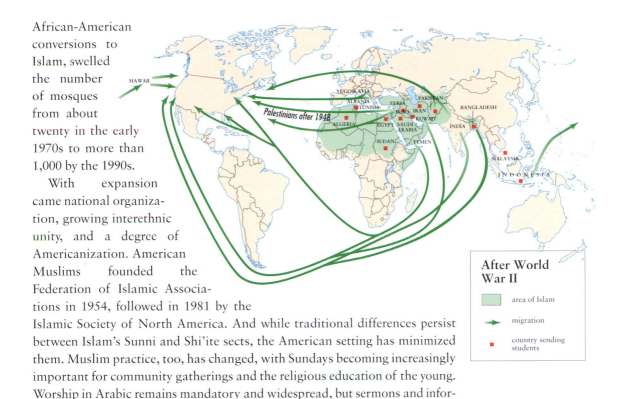

After World War II

- area of Islam
- → migration
- ■ country sending students

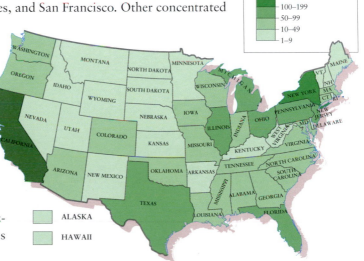

Islam mosques by state, 2000

- over 200
- 100–199
- 50–99
- 10–49
- 1–9

Hinduism and Sikhism in America

Hinduism, a range of polytheistic religious variations on basic common themes, came to America largely through 20th-century trans-Pacific migrations from India and other parts of south Asia, first to California and Hawaii and then to places across the country. Its core belief is that an impersonal spiritual Absolute descends into such deities as Vishnu, Shiva, and Krishna—statues of whom are objects of ritual devotion in temples and homes—and exists as a spark within each individual that can be realized through meditative yoga with the aid of a guru. Each region of India reveres particular deities and has developed particular yogic practices.

Hinduism first became significant in America as an "export" religion, presented by Hindu missionaries and popularized by American Transcendentalists and Theosophists during the mid- to late 19th century. It was decisively established by Hindu missionary Swami Vivekananda (1863–1902). After appearing at the 1893 World's Parliament of Religions in Chicago, where he stressed the fundamental unity of Hinduism, Buddhism, and Christianity, he toured the nation twice and established the Vedanta Society, with centers in San Francisco, New York, and other cities, to promote Hinduism in a Western context. It eventually established headquarters in Los Angeles. Largely limited in its appeal to urban middle-class whites—though more recently attracting ethnic Indians—its thirteen centers serve about 1,500 members. Another Hindu export—more fully devoted to guru-led yoga techniques—was developed by Paramahansa Yogananda (1893–1952), who arrived in America in 1920 and established the Self-Realization Fellowship (SRF) in Los Angeles in 1925. Combining Hinduism, Christianity, and a practical emphasis on personal health and power, he achieved enduring influence among liberal middle-class

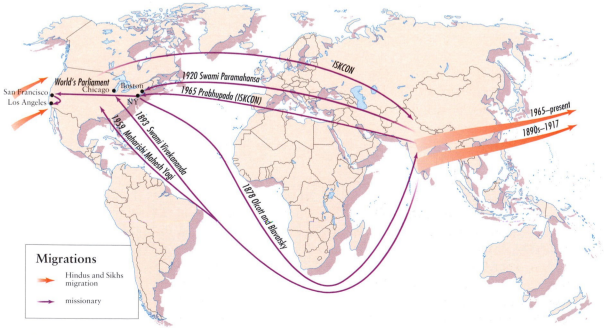

Migrations

→ Hindus and Sikhs migration

→ missionary

Hindu temples, 1994

white Christians. The SRF claimed 200,000 members by 1960, and by 1990 had eight temples (seven in California) and about 150 centers nationwide. Its Church of All Religions blends Christian and Hindu scriptures in Sunday services.

Westernized Hinduism expanded further among white Americans amid the countercultural religious ferment of the 1960s and 1970s. Among the more successful of the many new Hindu-based movements was Transcendental Meditation (TM), which emphasizes the achievement of personal relaxation and happiness through yoga and was brought to America in 1959 by the Maharishi Mahesh Yogi (b. 1911?). Having founded the International Meditation Society in India, he made several tours of the United States, establishing the Students' International Meditation Society in 1966 and hundreds of local meditation centers. TM's individualistic thrust and promise of personal fulfillment helped it enter American middle-class culture, particularly as economic and political unease mounted during the 1970s. It established no strong institutions in America, but TM centers exist in most major American cities. Another particularly successful Hindu movement, smaller but tighter, was the International Society for Krishna Consciousness (ISKCON). Founded in New York in 1966 by Abhay Charanaravinda Bhaktivedanta Swami Prabhupada (1896–1977), it soon relocated to San Francisco—a countercultural center— and then to Los Angeles. ISKCON's monotheistic devotion to Krishna departs from traditional Hinduism, but its devotional practices—including chanting of Krishna's name, temple rituals, and asceticism—are more like those of ethnic Indian Hinduism than those of other "export" versions. Most adherents live in urban settings, but ISKCON maintains seven farming communities. Its following, initially white and middle-class, has been small—about 3,000 people in more than sixty temples by the early 1990s—but its recent appeal to Indian immigrants has brought financial stability, moved it further toward "ethnic" Hinduism, and aided its missionary efforts in India.

The "ethnic" Hinduism of Asian Indians came to America as early as 1820, but significant numbers first arrived in the late 1890s, mostly from northwestern India, seeking railroad jobs in the Pacific states. Most eventually entered agriculture. Exclusionary legislation kept Indian immigration small—it totaled only about 12,000 by 1960. These early immigrants concentrated in California, constructing only two temples (San Francisco and Los Angeles) and sometimes worshiping in Vedanta centers. But hundreds of thousands of Asian Indians arrived after the 1965 relaxation of immigration restrictions. Generally prosperous, highly educated, and uneasy with perceived American decadence, they expanded ethnic Hinduism, practicing the devotions of their respective religions in their homes and, by the 1970s, founding temples nationwide. Between 1986 and the early 1990s—by which time the number of Indian Americans approached 850,000—the number of Hindu temples rose from forty to more than 150. Where Indian populations are large, as in New York, these temples perpetuate the Asian pattern of devotion to specific regional deities, but temples serving smaller populations have abandoned that pattern in favor of ecumenism in order to accommodate the diverse deities and practices of their supporters.

Sikh gurdwara, Hughson, California. Sikhs arrived on America's Pacific coast and established enduring communities in California's agricultural Central Valley.

Gurabo, PUERTO RICO
Honolulu, HAWAII

"Export" Hinduism

- Vedanta locale
- ISKCON locale
- Self-Realization locale

Not all Asian Indian immigrants were Hindu. Indian Muslims established a mosque in Stockton, California, by 1945, and Jains from northwest India brought their ascetic lifestyles and Hindu-like devotions. But a larger number—indeed, most of the first wave of Indian immigration in the 1890s—were Sikhs, followers of a monotheistic and Islam-inspired reform of Hinduism. Arriving in California, Sikhs formed significant, often insulated communities in its rural central valley and opened their first *gurdwara* (temple) in Stockton in 1909. Immigration restrictions in 1917 halted immigration, and a second temple (El Centro, California) did not appear until 1948. But expanding Sikh immigration after 1965 raised the nation's Sikh population to about 250,000 by the mid-1990s and carried *gurdwaras* beyond California to large cities nationwide—though more than half are still in California.

Buoyed by rising immigration and Western spiritual searching, Hinduism and Sikhism became firmly established on the American religious landscape during the 20th century.

Buddhism in America

Buddhism, like Hinduism, arrived from Asia, evolved in America as a multifarious tradition, and assumed both "ethnic" forms practiced by Asian immigrants and their descendants and "export" forms adopted by non-Asian Americans seeking religious alternatives. Following the geographic patterns of Asian immigration and the American counterculture, it has concentrated on the West Coast and elsewhere, mostly in urban areas. We shall consider some of its largest and most visible American forms.

Buddhism promotes "right" living and spiritual enlightenment, often through meditation. It originated in India in the 6th century BCE, spread across Asia after the 1st century CE, and developed into variant forms. Theravada, a nontheistic system emphasizing the historical Buddha as a spiritual model for humanity, came to dominate in southern Asia. The larger Mahayana school became dominant in China and Japan, producing a polytheistic belief system by emphasizing the spiritual potential in everyone and divinizing those who realize it. A third school, Vajrayana, developed later and flourished in Tibet. Each school developed numerous variants.

White Americans became aware of Buddhism through the Asian trade in the late 18th century, and it was studied by 19th-century Transcendentalists and Theosophists, but it became a significant American presence only when about 300,000 Chinese immigrants became laborers in California during and after the gold rush. They established their first temple in San Francisco in 1853, some

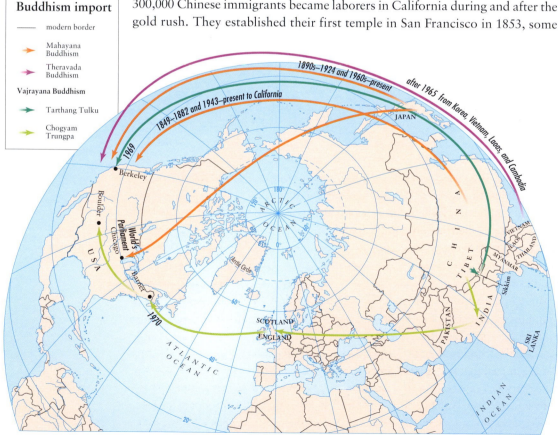

Buddhism import

——	modern border
→	Mahayana Buddhism
→	Theravada Buddhism

Vajrayana Buddhism

→	Tarthang Tulku
→	Chogyam Trungpa

400 shrines along the Pacific coast by 1900, and, adapting the term "Dios" (God) from the region's Hispanic Catholics, countless "joss houses." But Chinese Buddhism's impact was limited by its frequent combination with Daoism and Confucianism, its practice largely in private (producing few formal institutions), and exclusionary legislation in 1882, which curtailed Chinese immigration and prompted the disappearance of the original temples. The 1943 repeal of this legislation caused a renewal of Chinese Buddhism in America, primarily on the West Coast. Perhaps its most influential expressions, both based in San Francisco, are Buddha's Universal Church (1963), serving mostly Chinese Americans, and the monastic, mostly white Sino-American Buddhist Association.

The Japanese have been far more influential in American Buddhism. They began arriving in the late 19th century, first in the Pacific states, later and more gradually in the East. They brought with them two Mahayana forms dominant in Japan and destined to become the largest in the United States: Jodo Shinshu (True Pure Land), which teaches that reverential chanting of Amida Buddha's name facilitates rebirth into a Pure Land and a state of transcendence, and Nichiren Shoshu, which promotes enlightenment through meditative worship and chanting on a text called the Lotus Sutra. Jodo Shinshu missionaries arrived in Hawaii in 1889 (before U.S. annexation) and in San Francisco in 1898, opening temples in both places, followed by two priests who in 1899 founded the Buddhist Mission of North America (BMNA) in San Francisco. The BMNA spread rapidly among Japanese immigrants but, despite its Americanizing impulses, was stunted by the 1924 Japanese Exclusion Act. The incarceration of Japanese Americans in Western "relocation" centers during World War II stimulated the BMNA to seek greater acceptance by becoming the Buddhist Churches of America (BCA) in 1944, and adopting Sunday services, Sunday schools, and various trappings of Protestant worship. The BCA became one of the nation's largest Buddhist organizations after the war. Today it has about 100,000 members, mostly Japanese American, and about a hundred temples, three-quarters of them in the Pacific states.

Nichiren Shoshu, less church-oriented and more evangelistic, arrived much later, in 1960, when Japanese immigrants established the Nichiren Shoshu of America (later, Nichiren Shoshu Academy) in California. Initially confined to ethnic Japanese, it recruited young non-Asians during the spiritual experimentation of the 1960s, attracting blacks and Latinos as well as whites. By 1967, about 95 percent of converts were non-Asian, and by 1970 it claimed 200,000 members in 258 chapters. Membership crested in the 1970s and early 1980s, and the NSA remains America's largest Buddhist group. It now claims 300,000 members, remains heavily non-Asian in composition, and is highly Americanized in its religious practices. It is based in Santa Monica, California, and maintains forty centers nationwide, with temples in Honolulu and in Etiwanda, California, as well as in New York, Chicago, and Washington, D.C.

Zen, America's best known and most strongly meditative Buddhist

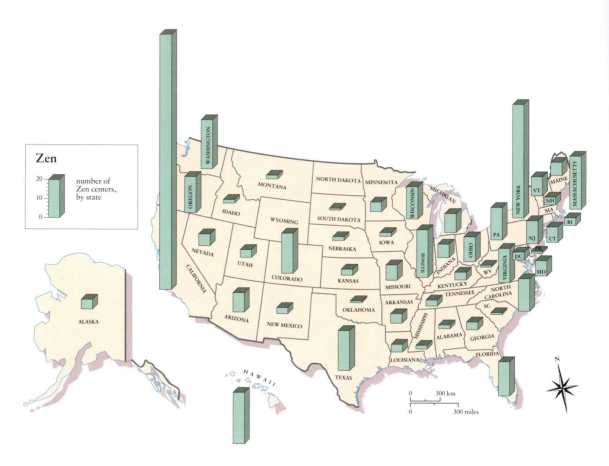

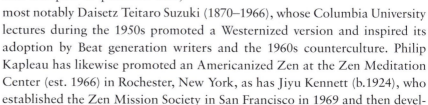

tradition, has been largely an export form throughout its American history, practiced by some Japanese immigrants but mostly by well-educated whites. It originated in China and developed in Japan into two forms: Rinzai, which wrenches the mind from ordinary consciousness through imponderable riddles, and Soto, which emphasizes gradual enlightenment and mental tranquility. Zen Buddhism was introduced to Americans at the World's Parliament of Religions in Chicago in 1893 by Rinzai missionary SoyEn Shaku (1859–1919), who made two subsequent lecture tours. He then sent several disciples to publicize Zen, most notably Daisetz Teitaro Suzuki (1870–1966), whose Columbia University lectures during the 1950s promoted a Westernized version and inspired its adoption by Beat generation writers and the 1960s counterculture. Philip Kapleau has likewise promoted an Americanized Zen at the Zen Meditation Center (est. 1966) in Rochester, New York, as has Jiyu Kennett (b.1924), who established the Zen Mission Society in San Francisco in 1969 and then developed a feministic Zen at the Shasta Abbey, founded in northern California in 1970. Shigemitsu Sasaki (1882–1945) promoted more traditional versions at Rinzai centers in California and New York and through the Buddhist Society in America (later renamed the First Zen Institute of America), established in New York in 1931. Soto practitioner Shunryu Suzuki (1904–71) has done likewise at his San Francisco Zen Center, established in 1961 and now the largest such center in America. Today there are hundreds of Zen centers and temples throughout the United States, mostly in cities, devoted to Korean and Vietnamese as well as Chinese and Japanese forms.

Tibetan Buddhism, a ritualistic tradition centering on gurus and promoting meditative contemplation through mantra chanting and mandala diagrams, is an important recent arrival. Its American presence as an export religion has grown since the 1960s through the work of missionaries who fled Tibet after the 1959 Chinese takeover. Tarthang Tulku (b. 1932?) established the Nyingma Meditation Center in Berkeley, California, after arriving there in 1969, and Chogyam Trungpa (1939–87), who arrived in 1970, founded Tibetan centers in cities across the country. In 1973 he established Vajradhatu, now the nation's largest Tibetan Buddhist organization. Tibetan centers of several varieties can now be found in most major American cities.

Buddhism is not the only major east Asian religious tradition in the United States. Many ethnic Chinese continue to combine it with Confucianism and Daoism, and Japanese Americans continue to practice Shinto. But Buddhism's institutionalization, urban focus, and interethnic appeal have made it the most highly visible east Asian tradition on an increasingly pluralistic American religious scene.

Buddhist Churches of America (BCA)

→ Buddhist immigration from Japan

▲ 1 BCA locale

● 1 BCA mission

PART VI: RELIGIONS OF THE MODERN AGE

American life was transformed in the late 19th and 20th centuries by a series of forces sometimes termed "modernization." These years witnessed the expansion of industrial production, mechanized large-scale agriculture, national institutional bureaucracies, and the nation's transportation and communications systems, resulting in an increasingly integrated transcontinental economy and civilization. Other important developments included the increasing immigration from farms and small towns to the expanding cities, the emergence of the United States as a major international power, and a series of intellectual revolutions that produced new theories of human nature. Against this backdrop formed new and combinative religious movements that sometimes incorporated and sometimes resisted these changes.

"Modernism" was the name often applied to an emergent liberal Protestantism shaped by the rise of Darwinian biology, psychoanalysis, and the social sciences and embraced in particular by Northern urban ministers and their middle-class parishioners. It approached the Bible through a "higher criticism" that challenged the traditional literal interpretation and assumed Scripture to be a product of historically located human beings rather than divine inspiration. It also rejected Calvinist notions of human sinfulness, teaching instead human goodness, the humanity of Jesus, and the responsibility of the church to address the ills of an urban industrial society.

An 1869 photograph of National Camp Meeting Association for the promotion of Holiness. The Holiness Movement urged intense personal religious experience as an antidote to institutionalized Methodism.

But modernism and modernization generated profound spiritual unease and provoked strong religious responses, including Protestant Fundamentalism, Holiness movements, and Pentecostalism, which emphasized timeless tradition, strict morality, an intense personal relationship with Jesus, and (in the case of Holiness and Pentecostalism) ecstatic worship. These movements found enthusiastic acceptance in the rural South, Midwest, and Central Plains, where the industrializing and diverse cities of the Northeast were perceived as threatening to traditional ways of life, and in the cities themselves, where many residents alienated by their social circumstances or by fashionable middle-class churches turned to storefront churches. In the South in particular—less thoroughly urbanized, largely avoided by immigrants, and thus more uniformly Anglo-Protestant than other parts of the nation—conservative Protestantism became intricately tied to a distinct regional identity. Ongoing tension between liberal and conservative groups became one of the most salient facets of 20th-century Protestantism.

Perhaps the most thoroughly disaffected people in urban America were the several million African Americans who followed a

"Great Migration" northward to the cities of the Northeast and Midwest during the early 20th century to seek alternatives to sharecropping and Jim Crow segregation. Transferred from rural poverty to urban poverty, from Southern racism to Northern racism, they looked to religion, sometimes to Christianity and sometimes beyond. Among Northern urban black neighborhoods, New York City's Harlem became a particularly important center of black culture, consciousness, and spiritual searching.

Further spiritual anxieties beset America after World War II. Despite—and because of—the nation's economic prosperity, suburbanization, superpower status, and Cold War claims to superiority over the "godless" Soviet Union, questions arose in the 1950s about its spiritual and moral fabric. Such reassessments intensified during the 1960s, as manifest in the civil rights movement, the identity movements it inspired among women, homosexuals, Latinos, and Native Americans, protests over the war in Vietnam, and the rise of an experimental youth counterculture, and during the 1970s, when the nation was humiliated by defeat in Vietnam, the Watergate affair, a faltering economy, and foreign policy crises in the Middle East. Some turned to Eastern religions, to psychological potential movements, or to eclectic New Age combinations of metaphysical, occult, and mystical elements in search of personal spiritual fulfillment and empowerment. Others sought new lives of moral discipline and personal commitment in strong, supportive, spiritual communities. These responses were especially pronounced in California, popular among spiritual seekers since the 19th century.

Marcus Garvey, founder of UNIA. Garvey's racial pride movement influenced many militant African American religious movements of the 20th century.

Still others turned to conservative Protestantism in recoil from what they perceived as an increasing moral and sexual permissiveness. This response was particularly salient in the Sunbelt—an area that stretches from Florida through the Desert Southwest to southern California and that experienced tremendous demographic expansion after World War II—but was apparent nationwide. This development can be glimpsed in part through statistics. Church membership dropped in such liberal denominations as the Episcopal Church (down 14.5 percent between 1960 and 1982), the United Church of Christ (down 23.4 percent), the Presbyterian Church (down 21.4 percent), and the United Methodist Church (down 11.6 percent). But membership in conservative and Pentecostal denominations surged in this period, the Southern Baptist Convention by 43.7 percent, the Assemblies of God by 120.1 percent, and the Church of God (Cleveland, Tennessee) by 172.5 percent.

Developments on the American religious scene during the 20th century, particularly during its latter third, leave little doubt of its vitality, dynamism, and expanding diversity as the 21st century dawns.

Fundamentalist Protestantism

Fundamentalism is often associated with the South but its key roots lay elsewhere. At Princeton Seminary, conservative Presbyterians resistant to the theory of biological evolution and innovations in biblical interpretation defended the literal truth of the Bible and such doctrines as Jesus's virgin birth and Resurrection. From England came "dispensational premillennialism," which divided human history into biblically defined epochs or "dispensations" and anticipated the return of Jesus to inaugurate the millennium, followed by the cataclysmic end of time. These doctrines were spread nationwide by a network of evangelists and Bible institutes centered on Dwight L. Moody (1837–99) and his Chicago institute and, after 1876, through an annual interdenominational conference series at Niagara, New York.

Fundamentalism became a distinct movement after World War I when its advocates became increasingly outspoken in their resistance to moderates and liberals in their denominations. They formed the World Christian Fundamentals Association in 1919 and, failing to seize control of the Disciples of Christ and the northern branches of the Presbyterian and Baptist denominations, established the General Association of Regular Baptists (1932), Conservative Baptist Association of America (1947), Orthodox Presbyterian Church (1936), and Bible Presbyterian Church (1937). Fundamentalism found a particularly congenial home in the South, in part because of the prevalence of Baptists and other evangelical denominations in the region; in part because fundamentalist strategies and commitments meshed with Baptist traditions of congregationalism, antiecclesiasticism, and adult baptism; and in part because many Southern religious conservatives perceived defense of evangelical tradition against evolution and other "Northern" innovations as a badge of regional pride.

Perhaps the most sensational expression of early fundamentalism, the 1925 Scopes trial, in which Fundamentalists successfully but embarrassingly defended a state law outlawing the teaching of evolution in

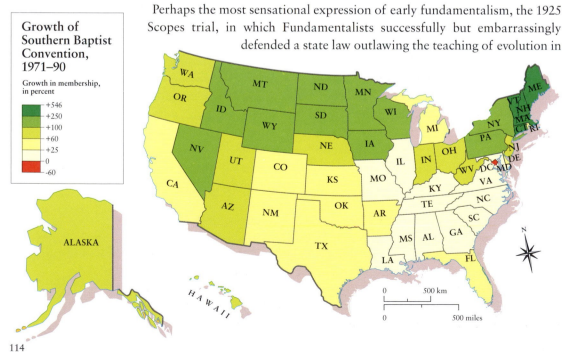

Growth of Southern Baptist Convention, 1971–90

Growth in membership, in percent

- +546
- +250
- +100
- +60
- +25
- 0
- -60

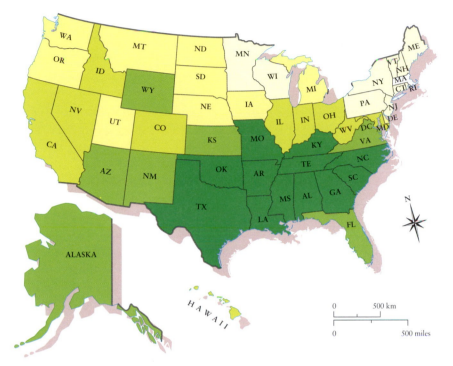

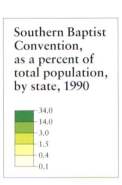

Southern Baptist
Convention,
as a percent of
total population,
by state, 1990

— 34.0
— 14.0
— 3.0
— 1.5
— 0.4
— 0.1

public schools, occurred in Dayton, Tennessee. Still, the movement was national in scope: some fifty fundamentalist Bible institutes dotted the country by 1930, and radio shows broadcast to large regional and national audiences from New York, Chicago, Los Angeles, and Fort Worth.

Fundamentalism faded from public view after the Scopes trial, but experienced institutional consolidation and a proliferation of independent congregations during the 1930s and assumed a new visibility after World War II as a result of Billy Graham's crusades across the nation. The cultural dislocations and political unrest of the 1960s and 1970s prompted a major fundamentalist resurgence that gave the movement a new national prominence and was especially pronounced in the South and the demographically expansive Sunbelt states. An explosion of television ministries in Virginia, North Carolina, and southern California attracted national audiences, huge independent Baptist "megachurches" became prominent features of the landscape in the South and elsewhere, and the presidencies of "born-again" Southern Baptist Jimmy Carter and California conservative Ronald Reagan signaled fundamentalism's powerful new political presence.

Fundamentalism's recent surge is apparent in the growth of the Southern Baptist Convention, which came decisively under fundamentalist control in the 1970s and became increasingly outspoken thereafter. Its growth since 1971 has been impressive not only numerically—though its 15.7 million members in the mid-1990s made it by far the nation's largest Protestant denomination—but geographically, coming in significant part through the affiliation of congregations outside the South. Its Christian traditionalism is not merely regional but national.

Holiness and Pentecostalism

Holiness and Pentecostalism, related but distinct conservative Protestant movements, developed around the turn of the 20th century in an attempt to preserve experiential piety against the modernization of American life. Holiness emerged among Methodists resisting their denomination's institutionalism and urban decorum, Pentecostalism among poorer urban and rural folk of evangelical background feeling threatened by urbanization and industrialization. Both experienced increasing denominational respectability during the 20th century.

The Holiness movement began amid the Second Great Awakening when, beginning in 1837, Phoebe Palmer (1807–74) sought to renew Methodism's original emphasis on "entire sanctification" (freedom from sin) in a weekly "Tuesday Meeting for the Promotion of Holiness" held in her New York City home. These meetings inspired similar ones, first in other Northeastern cities and then nationwide. There were some 200 by 1886. Holiness groups initially remained within the Methodist denomination, but their schismatic potential erupted early and powerfully in New York's burned-over district, where the Wesleyan Methodist Church emerged in Utica in 1843 and the Free Methodist Church in Pekin in 1860.

Holiness became more vigorous after the Civil War. A camp meeting held in Vineland, New Jersey, in 1867 sparked the formation of the National Camp Meeting Association for the Promotion of Holiness, which organized fifty-two camp meetings by 1883. During the 1870s and 1880s, the association expanded from Eastern urban areas into the rural Midwest, South, and Southwest, where newer rural groups already mistrustful of Northeastern industrialism resisted attempts by Northeastern Methodist authorities to curb their emotional worship, faith healing, and premillennialism. Nor did poor and working-class urban converts warm to Methodist leaders' middle-class decorum. The resulting tensions generated seces-

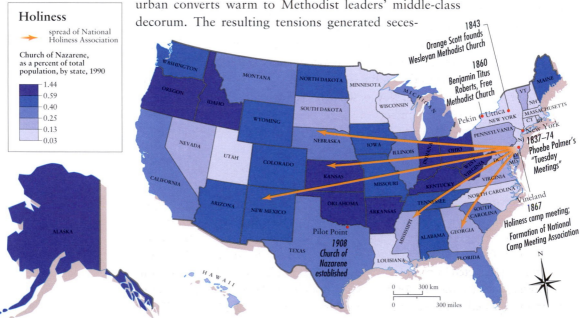

Holiness

→ spread of National Holiness Association

Church of Nazarene, as a percent of total population, by state, 1990

- 1.44
- 0.59
- 0.40
- 0.25
- 0.13
- 0.03

1843
Orange Scott founds
Wesleyan Methodist Church

1860
Benjamin Titus
Roberts, Free
Methodist Church

1837–74
Phoebe Palmer's
"Tuesday
Meetings"

1867
Holiness camp meeting;
Formation of National
Camp Meeting Association

1908
Church of
Nazarene
established

Pekin

Utica

Vineland

Pilot Point

0   300 km
0   300 miles

National Holiness
camp meetings,
1867–94

● one meeting

● two or more
meetings

sions and
expulsions from the
denomination and the
proliferation of independent
Holiness congregations, which
by the early 20th century began coalescing into new denominations.

The first of these was the Church of God (Anderson, Indiana), which emphasized faith healing and was established in 1880. Despite its early antidenominational thrust, it became a major denomination and now has more than 200,000 members, concentrated in the Midwest, southern Plains, and South. Another important denomination, the Pilgrim Holiness Church, emerged in 1922 when the International Apostolic Holiness Church merged with like-minded denominations. In 1968, it in turn merged with the Wesleyan Methodist Church to form the Wesleyan Church, which now has about 110,000 members, largely in the Midwest and South. The largest Holiness body is the Church of the Nazarene, formed at Pilot Point, Texas, in 1908 through a merger of two urban groups—an identically named church founded in Los Angeles in 1895 and the Eastern-based Association of Pentecostal Churches, established in 1896—with the Holiness Church of Christ, an organization of rural Southern congregations. Now based in Kansas City, Missouri, the Church grew from about 35,000 members in seventy-eight congregations in 1915 to about 575,000 members in 5,175 congregations in 1990. Its largest numbers are in the Midwest, the Plains, and the West.

Pentecostalism emerged from the Holiness movement in 1901 at the Bethel Bible College, founded in 1900 in Topeka, Kansas, by Holiness evangelist Charles F. Parham (1873–1937). Having decided that speaking in tongues, experienced by the apostles on the day of Pentecost, was the definitive indicator of what Holiness advocates called "Spirit baptism" and a sign of Christ's imminent return, Parham encouraged the experience among his students. Parham's doctrine was rejected by most Holiness advocates, but he sparked a brief revival in southeastern Kansas. By 1905 he had founded an "Apostolic Faith" movement and opened a Bible school in Houston, Texas. In 1906, black Holiness

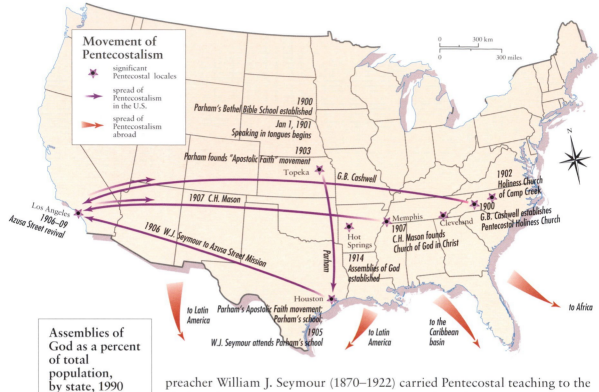

Movement of Pentecostalism

- significant Pentecostal locales
- spread of Pentecostalism in the U.S.
- spread of Pentecostalism abroad

1900
Parham's Bethel Bible School established

Jan 1, 1901
Speaking in tongues begins

1903
Parham founds "Apostolic Faith" movement
Topeka

G.B. Cashwell

1902
Holiness Church of Camp Creek

1900
G.B. Cashwell establishes Pentecostal Holiness Church

1907 C.H. Mason

Los Angeles
1906–09
Azusa Street revival

1906 W.J. Seymour to Azusa Street Mission

Memphis
Cleveland

1907
C.H. Mason founds Church of God in Christ

Hot Springs

Parham

1914
Assemblies of God established

to Latin America

Houston
Parham's Apostolic Faith movement; Parham's school;

1905
W.J. Seymour attends Parham's school

to Latin America

to the Caribbean basin

to Africa

Assemblies of God as a percent of total population, by state, 1990

- 2.83
- 1.35
- 1.00
- 0.71
- 0.48
- 0.12

preacher William J. Seymour (1870–1922) carried Pentecostal teaching to the black Holiness Azusa Street mission in Los Angeles, where he presided over a three-year-long revival that attracted blacks, whites, Asians, Mexicans, and others. Visitors to Azusa Street brought its message to the rural South and Midwest, where they attracted Holiness, Baptist, and Methodist groups and founded new denominations. Flourishing where Holiness did—particularly southern Appalachia, the Ozarks, the coastal and piedmont areas of the Carolinas and Georgia, the central and southern Plains, and in urban storefronts in Los Angeles and elsewhere—Pentecostalism produced more than 300 denominations, most small but some quite large.

The oldest is the Church of God in Christ, founded in 1897 as a Holiness denomination but converted to Pentecostalism by Holiness-Baptist minister Charles H. Mason (1866–1961) of Memphis, Tennessee, after he visited Azusa Street. The world's largest black Pentecostal church, it established early strongholds in the South and southern Plains and in 1993 claimed 6 million members in more than 15,000 congregations. Another large Pentecostal denomination, and the second-oldest, is the Church of God (Cleveland, Tennessee). Established in 1907, it originated as the Holiness Church of Camp Creek, formed in

1902 by revival-fired Baptist groups in eastern Tennessee and western North Carolina. Its 1990 report of about 620,000 members in more than 5,800 congregations shows that the church has spread from North Carolina and Tennessee to broader regional reach in the South and Midwest. The sizable Pentecostal Holiness Church, International resulted from a 1911 merger between a North Carolina group of that name, led by another Azusa participant, and the Fire-Baptized Holiness Church, founded in South Carolina in 1898 as a union among several Holiness groups in the Southern and Plains states. Originally based in Georgia, the church moved to Oklahoma City in 1973, remains strongest in the South and the Plains, and reported about 120,000 members in 1990. The world's largest white Pentecostal denomination is the Assemblies of God, the product of a 1914 merger in Hot Springs, Arkansas, among groups in Texas, Oklahoma, Alabama, and Illinois. It grew during the 20th century from its founding membership of 6,000 to 2.2 million nationwide—with its strongest representation in the states of the Plains and Sunbelt—and 25 million worldwide. Concerns with charlatanism led it to overcome its initial resistance to formal organization, and its membership became increasingly affluent after World War II, contradicting popular images of Pentecostalism as purely a religion of the poor and disinherited.

Indeed, Pentecostal and Holiness churches generally—especially the larger ones, and especially since about 1970—have acculturated toward normative middle-class American life and spread beyond their early regional bases to become national in scope. They have enjoyed growing appeal, often in storefront settings, among Latino Americans, Korean Americans, and other recent immigrant groups, and have achieved global reach through successful missionizing in Latin America, the Caribbean Basin, Africa, and Asia.

Church of God (Cleveland) as a percent of total population, by state, 1990

- 1.49
- 0.40
- 0.15
- 0.09
- 0.05
- 0.01

Church of God in Christ as a percent of religious membership, by state, 1936

- 0.38
- 0.10
- 0.05
- 0.03
- 0.005
- 0.00

Urban African-American Religions

African Americans migrating from the rural South to the cities of the Northeast and Midwest to escape economic hardship and racial discrimination found more of both. They sought personal wholeness, collective spiritual identity, and economic mobility through a range of religious responses to the alienating circumstances of urban life.

Most looked to Christianity, especially its evangelical and ecstatic forms. The black Baptist, Methodist, Holiness, and Pentecostal denominations flourished in urban storefronts, and sometimes encouraged racial pride and militancy by postulating a black God and advocating emigration to the sacred homeland of Africa. Another movement connected to Christianity was the Universal Negro Improvement Association (UNIA), founded in Jamaica by Marcus Garvey (1887–1940) in 1914 and relocated to Harlem after Garvey emigrated there in 1916. Attracting African Americans amid the urban racial violence of the late 1910s, the UNIA had grown in the United States to more than 2 million members in thirty chapters—mostly in California and the Eastern half of the nation—by 1919. Through meetings, rituals, small businesses, a newspaper, ties with black churches, a proposed Black Star steamship line, and an anthem ("Ethiopia, Thou Land of Our Fathers"), its members pursued economic and

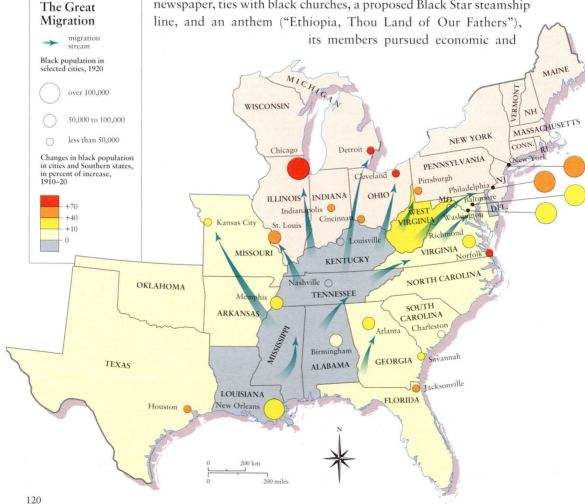

The Great Migration

→ migration stream

Black population in selected cities, 1920

◯ over 100,000

◯ 50,000 to 100,000

◯ less than 50,000

Changes in black population in cities and Southern states, in percent of increase, 1910–20

+70
+40
+10
0

cultural separatism and an eventual return to Africa. The UNIA also supported the African Orthodox Church, founded in 1921 in New York City by Antiguan immigrant, militant Anglican priest, and UNIA chaplain George A. McGuire (1886–1934). The UNIA faltered after Garvey's Black Star venture led to his imprisonment and deportation to Jamaica in 1927, and collapsed when Harlem leaders resisted Garvey's attempt to move its headquarters to Kingston. But its ideology greatly influenced subsequent black militancy in America.

The most militant religious movements rejected Christianity in favor of other traditions considered more suitable to African-American identity. Some urban blacks considered ancient Hebrews their ancestors and—finding support in the existence of Ethiopia's "Falasha" Jews—viewed Judaism as their true religion. UNIA choirmaster Arnold J. Ford (1890?–1935?) founded Beth B'nai Abraham in Harlem in 1924 and in 1930 emigrated to Ethiopia. He passed the organization to Wentworth A. Matthew (1892–1973), who had already established the Commandment Keepers Congregation of the Living God in Harlem in 1919. Another group, the Original Hebrew Israelite Nation, combined Orthodox Judaism and black nationalism. A Chicago Israelite group emigrated to Israel in 1970, and while many returned to America after the Israeli government refused to recognize their Judaism, some remained in a Negev settlement. Least Judaic is the Church of God and Saints of Christ, established in Lawrence, Kansas, in 1896. Combining Christianity, Judaism, and black nationalism, it moved first to Philadelphia (1900) and then to Belleville, Virginia, its current home, where it grew into the largest black Hebrew sect. Historically strongest in Chicago, black Hebrew groups experienced a growth spurt

Garveyist movement

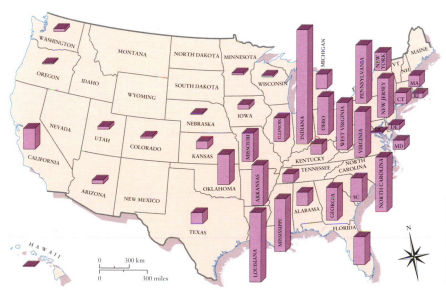

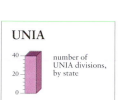

UNIA

number of UNIA divisions, by state

Black Hebrew organizations

amid the black consciousness movements of the early 1970s but have declined in membership since.

Far more important in the development of black religious identity in the 20th century have been Islamic movements. The first was Moorish Science, founded by Noble Drew Ali (1866– 1929). Born Timothy Drew in North Carolina, he migrated to Newark, New Jersey, where he founded the Moorish Holy Temple of Science in 1913. He taught that blacks were Asiatics and therefore Moors, or Muslims, and that his followers were to pray facing Mecca. Moorish Science differs from traditional Islam: its "Holy Koran," unlike the Qu'ran, combines Christianity, Islam, and Spiritualism, and its worship includes several Christian features. Still, Ali's point was that African-Americans seeking spiritual identity needed to look beyond Christianity. The movement spread from the cities of the Northeast to those of the Midwest and upper South, and temples appeared in Harlem, Detroit, Philadelphia, Pittsburgh, and several Southern cities. The movement was strongest in Chicago, where Ali established headquarters in 1925. At its height in the late 1920s, the movement encompassed nearly 30,000 members, with temples in at least fourteen cities. But it splintered after Drew's death, and only the Chicago and Hartford, Connecticut, temples remain active.

Many of Drew's followers in Detroit joined the Nation of Islam, founded there in 1929 by Wallace D. Fard (?–1934?), or Wali Farad Muhammad, whose problack and antiwhite variety of Islam, like Drew's, diverged from Muslim orthodoxy. Fard opened a temple in 1931, but he disappeared in 1934. The ensuing internal tensions drove to Chicago his chief follower, Elijah Muhammad (1897–1975), the son of a sharecropper and Baptist minister who had migrated to Detroit from Georgia in 1923. Muhammad established Temple Number 2 in 1936, and by 1950 assumed control of the movement. He attracted followers with a message that whites were inherently evil, that Christianity was an instrument of white oppression, and that moral discipline would allow blacks to achieve economic independence and control of their destiny. He also presided over the movement's rise to national prominence; it experienced spectacular growth as black militancy heightened in the late 1950s and early 1960s, reaching perhaps 500,000 members by 1963, and there were a hundred temples by the time of Muhammad's death. Particularly important to the Nation's success was Malcolm X (1925–65), born Malcolm Little, who became its national spokesman and established temples in Harlem (of which he became minister), Philadelphia, Boston, Atlanta, and on the West Coast.

But by 1964 he had broken with the Nation, made a pilgrimage to Mecca, converted to Orthodox Islam, and renounced racial separatism. These moves triggered his 1965 assassination.

Ironically, Elijah Muhammad's son, Wallace (later Warith) Deen Muhammad (b.1933), moved the Nation and most of its membership toward traditional Islam after his father's death, changing its name to the American Muslim Mission in 1980 and then dissolving it into the international Islamic community in 1985. A smaller faction led by Louis Farrakhan (b. 1933) retained the Nation's original name and message, but he has recently moderated his aggressive racial posture in such nationally publicized events as the Million Man March of 1995, and in his approach to rapprochement with Warith Deen Muhammad. The viability of this latter development remains unclear, but the permanence of African-American Islam—which accounted by the mid-1990s for some 3 million of America's 8 million Muslims—appears assured.

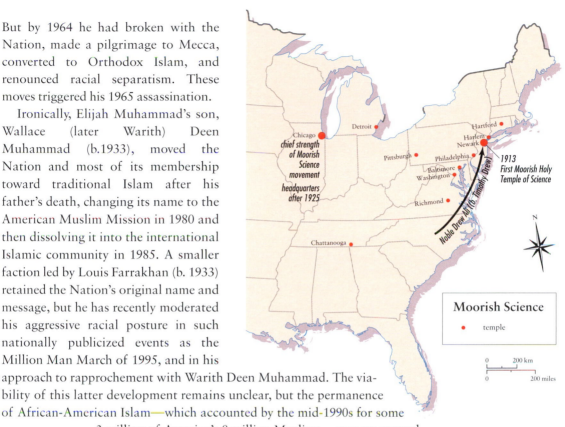

Moorish Science

• temple

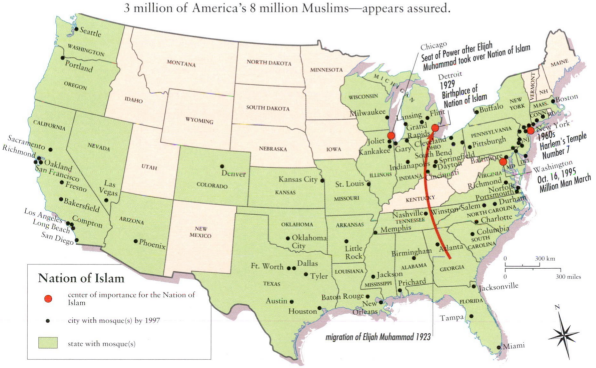

Nation of Islam

● center of importance for the Nation of Islam

• city with mosque(s) by 1997

▨ state with mosque(s)

123

Unificationism, Scientology, and Baha'i

The continuing expansion of American religious life in the 20th century was apparent in a plethora of new movements that combined Christian, non-Western, metaphysical, and healing traditions into novel forms. Three such movements—the Unification Church, Scientology, and Baha'i religion—illustrate these trends.

The Unification Church—officially called the Holy Spirit Association for the Unification of World Christianity—was founded in Korea by Sun Myung Moon (b. 1920). Born in what is now North Korea, Moon was nurtured in Korean religions and a Pentecostally infused Presbyterianism, became a Christian minister, and was imprisoned by North Korea's communist government. After being freed in 1953, he established the Unification Church and increasingly vocalized anticommunist views. Revelations he claimed from Jesus, Moses, Buddha, and others convinced him that God would send a new messiah—identified as Moon by his followers—to complete Jesus' mission of restoring the "perfect" family state lost in Eden. Unificationists conceived of their church in this light, calling each other "brothers" and "sisters" and Moon their spiritual "Father." Marriage, the key sacrament, is controlled by Moon, who promotes the unification of humanity by joining followers of differing cultural backgrounds in "group marriages" or mass weddings.

Moon began sending missionaries to the United States in 1959, and in the 1960s his message of the oneness of humanity, ascetic discipline, and strong community appealed to youth seeking an alternative to the counterculture. But the church experienced significant growth only after Moon immigrated to the United States in the early 1970s. Recruiting especially on college campuses, it attracted young, white, urban, well-educated, single, middle-class, mostly Northeastern Americans—even-

1959 Unification missionaries

from Korea

early 1970s arrival of Sun Myung Moon

Unification
- church

tually as many as 30,000 members—by offering spiritual grounding and quasi-familial ties amid the political, social, and economic turmoil of the 1970s. But outsiders criticized its group marriages and labeled it a dangerous "cult." The church in America suffered setbacks when Moon was imprisoned for tax evasion in 1982 and decided after his release to focus his efforts on Asia. Concerned to emphasize its socially and spiritually transformative function and end its public perception as a denomination, it dissolved and reorganized as the Family Federation for World Peace and Unification (USA) in 1997. Its current American membership of perhaps 5,000 to 10,000 remains mostly white, urban, Northeastern, and middle-class but increasingly middle-aged.

The Unification Church's sanctification of marriage and family, conveyed in this couple blessing, appealed to many young Americans seeking spiritual stability in the turbulent 1970s.

The Church of Scientology—offering a metaphysical "science" of healing based on Eastern and ancient Greek thought, modern occultism, and psychoanalytic theory—was organized by science fiction writer L. Ron Hubbard (1911–86) in 1953. Hubbard taught that personal wellness—and material and social success—requires a mentally "clear" state achieved by purging the mind of painful unconscious images or "engrams" accumulated in one's present and previous lives. This is done through consultation with "auditors" who use "E-meters" (electrometers) to detect engrams. Continued auditing can entirely liberate the individual's powerful spiritual essence, or "thetan." Scientology became a fad during the 1950s and, like Erhard Seminars Training (EST) and other therapeutic systems, surged amid the economic malaise of the 1970s. Churches appeared nationwide, especially—as with other American metaphysical movements—in urban areas and on the West Coast. It developed into a hierarchically arranged movement with an ordained ministry—it refers to auditors as pastoral counselors—and has sought legal recognition as a church. But it has aroused the opposition of mainline religions, the medical profession, and the governments of the United States, Great Britain, Australia, New Zealand, and (most recently) Germany. Public hostility drove Hubbard into isolation, sometimes at sea and sometimes in southern California, where the movement's institutional presence remains most concentrated. Based in Los Angeles, Scientology now maintains about 700 churches and claims 8 million members worldwide (critics set the figure at 50,000).

The Baha'i religion, established in Persia (now Iran) in 1863, is based on messianic and other aspects of Shi'ite Islam. Its founder, Husayn Ali

Scientology

● church

(1817–1892), called himself Baha'u'llah ("the glory of God"), claiming to be a divine messenger offering a new post-Islamic dispensation of unity and peace based on the oneness of God, of humanity, and of all religions. He modified such traditional Islamic practices as daily prayer, the annual month of fasting, pilgrimage, and almsgiving, and replaced the Qu'ran with a new scripture that combined the teachings of Islam with

Scientology

● mission

those of Judaism, Christianity, Buddhism, and the Middle Eastern religion of Zoroastrianism. (Hindu elements were later incorporated.) This scripture emphasizes spiritual growth, healing, racial and ethnic integration, gender equality, and universal justice.

Lebanese convert Ibrahim Khayru'llah brought the faith to the United States, arriving in Chicago in the aftermath of the World's Parliament of Religions and offering classes there beginning in 1894. The movement had attracted more than 700 adherents in the area by 1899, and continues to maintain its American mother temple in the Chicago suburb of Wilmette and its national headquarters in Evanston. But it spread to twenty-four states by 1900 and grew more effectively after an organizing campaign in the 1920s. Spectacular growth in numbers and ethnic diversity came in the 1960s because of the appeal of its integrationist message to the young; a proselytizing campaign in the rural South that recruited some 15,000 African-Americans from South Carolina and elsewhere; the arrival in the 1970s of thousands of Baha'i refugees from political turmoil in Vietnam, Laos, and Cambodia; and the flight of some 10,000 Iranian Baha'is, mostly to Los Angeles, after the 1979 Islamic revolution. Native and Latino Americans have also converted in growing numbers. The cumulative effect was that American membership rose from about 10,000 in 1963 to about 100,000 in 1987. By 2000, there were 137,000 American members in some 7,000 locales—with the largest number of both in California—and about 5 million members worldwide. Members shun partisan politics as antithetical to unity, but racial equality, social justice, and support for the United Nations remain paramount concerns of American Baha'is.

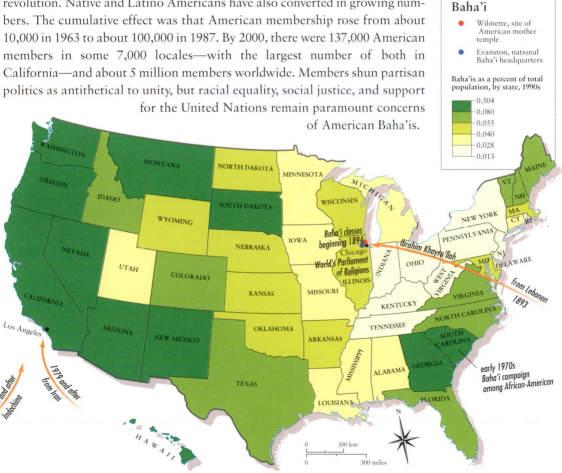

Baha'i

- 🔴 Wilmette, site of American mother temple
- 🔵 Evanston, national Baha'i headquarters

Baha'is as a percent of total population, by state, 1990s

- 0.504
- 0.080
- 0.055
- 0.040
- 0.028
- 0.013

EPILOGUE: AMERICAN RELIGIOUS REGIONS

Perhaps the most important concept in the study of the geography of American religion has been that of regionalism. The idea that different geographic sections of indigenous America, the English colonies, are the United States have been characterized by distinctive religious features has helped historians and cultural geographers to make sense of what might otherwise seem an overwhelmingly complex American religious scene.

Regional patterns developed even before the first European settlers arrived, for the variety of religious patterns created by Indian groups responded in part to local geographic and climatic features. Thus one can speak of "northern" and "southern" patterns, each in turn comprising many different kinds of belief and practice. Cultural anthropologists have distinguished several broad culture regions in pre-Columbian North America, each of which might well be considered a religious region as well.

European colonization brought new religious traditions to America that were less directly tied to American physical geography but nonetheless contributed important and enduring regional patterns to American religious life. The Russian Orthodoxy brought across the Bering Sea remains a major religious presence among Alaskan natives, far more prominent there than elsewhere in the United States, and Russian settlement, Orthodox and otherwise, continues to concentrate along the Pacific; the strength of Catholicism (both Mexican and Native American) in the American Southwest testifies to the continuing impact of Spanish colonialism on the American religious map; and French Catholic Louisiana remains as a vestige of France's once large Mississippi Valley presence.

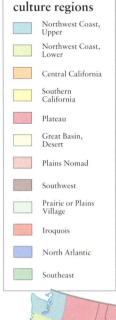

Native American culture regions

- Northwest Coast, Upper
- Northwest Coast, Lower
- Central California
- Southern California
- Plateau
- Great Basin, Desert
- Plains Nomad
- Southwest
- Prairie or Plains Village
- Iroquois
- North Atlantic
- Southeast

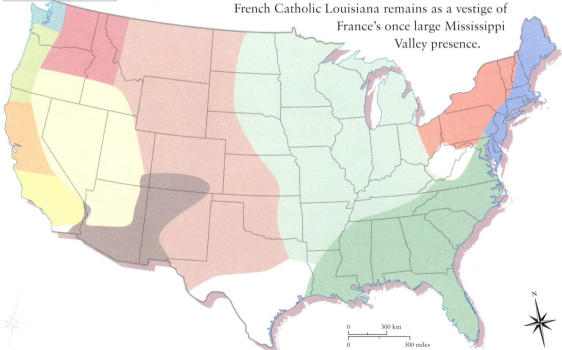

0   300 km

0   300 miles

American church historians have long noted that, in the English colonies, Puritan Congregationalism was concentrated in New England, Anglicanism (the forerunner of Episcopalianism) in Virginia, Maryland, New York, and Connecticut, Presbyterianism in the backcountry, Quakerism in Philadelphia and the Delaware Valley, and German groups in western Pennsylvania. Many of these patterns persist, though they have been overlain by newer ones and no longer define their respective regions.

During the 19th century, revivalism, religious innovation, immigration, and westward expansion produced new regional patterns that were clearly visible by 1900 and have formed the basis for the current American religious regions that scholars have widely—if cautiously and provisionally—recognized. Seven major regions and several subregions were suggested by cultural geographer Wilbur Zelinsky in 1961.

The first is *New England*, north and east of New York state, characterized by large numbers of Congregationalists, Unitarian-Universalists, Episcopalians, and Catholics and a relative lack of Methodist, Presbyterian, and German groups. The *Midland* region to its south stretches westward from the mid-Atlantic states to the Rocky Mountains. This territory, unlike *New England*, abounds in Methodists, Presbyterians, and German groups, as well as Baptists, Episcopalians, and Disciples of Christ. A *Pennsylvania German* subregion within it is heavily populated by Amish, Mennonite, and related groups. A third region, the *Upper Middle Western*, occupies the nation's middle third longitudinally and upper third latitudinally, encompassing the area extending westward from Lake Michigan through the Dakotas. Its distinguishing features, products of 19th-century

European colonization regions c. 1750

English influence	
French influence	
Russian influence	
Spanish influence	
	modern state boundaries shown for reference only

migration, immigration, and settlement, are the dominance of northern European Lutherans, a strong contingent of Catholics, and, due to westward migration from New England during the early part of the century, a significant Congregational presence. Baptists have predominated in the *Southern* region since the rise of evangelicalism in the 19th century, but Methodists have constituted a large minority since the same period, and Holiness and Pentecostal

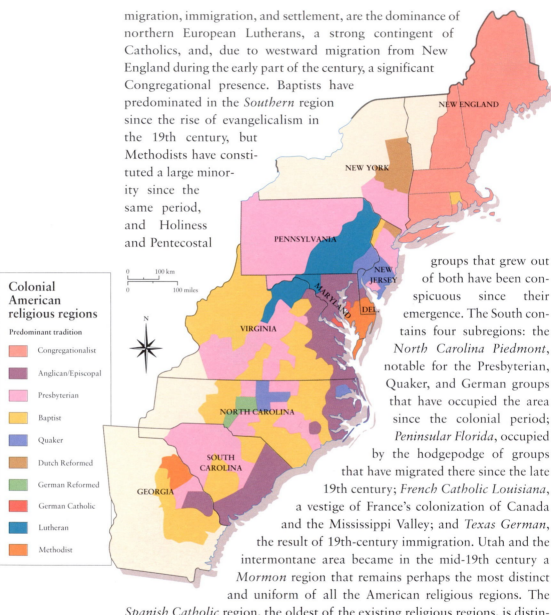

Colonial American religious regions

Predominant tradition

- Congregationalist
- Anglican/Episcopal
- Presbyterian
- Baptist
- Quaker
- Dutch Reformed
- German Reformed
- German Catholic
- Lutheran
- Methodist

groups that grew out of both have been conspicuous since their emergence. The South contains four subregions: the *North Carolina Piedmont*, notable for the Presbyterian, Quaker, and German groups that have occupied the area since the colonial period; *Peninsular Florida*, occupied by the hodgepodge of groups that have migrated there since the late 19th century; *French Catholic Louisiana*, a vestige of France's colonization of Canada and the Mississippi Valley; and *Texas German*, the result of 19th-century immigration. Utah and the intermontane area became in the mid-19th century a *Mormon* region that remains perhaps the most distinct and uniform of all the American religious regions. The *Spanish Catholic* region, the oldest of the existing religious regions, is distinguished, obviously, by its concentration of Catholics of Hispanic descent as well as of Native American Catholics, and points to the religious culture that predominates on the other side of the nation's nearby border with Mexico. The final region is the *Western*, which is like the Peninsular Florida subregion in being settled largely by migrants from other regions of the country and lacking any one clearly dominant group or cluster of dominant groups as a result.

The concept of American religious regions has its limitations. For one thing, other sorts of patterns coexist with and cut across them. Urban areas, for example, have been perennial exceptions to the general rules of their regions, while certain religious groups are notable for either a largely urban presence (such as Jews, Catholics, Episcopalians, and Unitarian-Universalists) or a largely rural one (Churches of God, Disciples of Christ, Baptists, Amish, and Mennonites). Another problem with the existing regional schema is that, having been sketched before 1965 changes in immigration laws stimulated trans-Pacific Asian migration and in the absence of reliable statistics on African-American denominations, they do not reflect the presence of these Americans. They are based on the increasingly inaccurate portrait of the United States as a nation of white Protestants, Catholics, and Jews. Perhaps the conventional schema can be stretched to incorporate the far more complex reality: accounting for black denominations, for example, might not change the Baptist-Methodist-Pentecostal definition of the South; Eastern Orthodoxy might simply be mixed into existing portraits of the Midlands and Upper Midwest; and the definition of the West, especially California, might be changed to include metaphysical religious movements, countercultural experimentation, and its Asian population. But perhaps such changes will require a more substantial redrawing of the map of American religious regions.

Finally, the enduring distinctiveness of the religious regions that took form during the 19th and 20th centuries appears less than certain at the dawn of the 21st. Many observers have suggested that mass culture, the mass media, and interregional migration have operated to homogenize American life and erase regional religious differences. Regional distinctiveness continues to have its defenders, but whether future atlases like this one treat American religious regions as anything more than a matter of historical interest remains to be seen.

Current religious regions

- New England
- Midland
- Pennsylvania German
- Upper Middle Western
- Southern
- Carolina Piedmont
- Peninsular Florida
- French Catholic
- Texas German
- Spanish Catholic
- Mormon
- Western
- principal Catholic concentration

Chronology

30,000 BCE	Siberian hunters enter North America.
3000 BCE	Adena and Hopewell civilizations.
500 BCE	Polynesian peoples first settle Hawaiian Islands.
1250 CE	Mississippi Valley civilization at its height.
1492	Spain expels Jews and Muslims; Columbus reaches Western Hemisphere.
1513	Spain establishes first Catholic church in Americas at San Juan, Puerto Rico.
1565	St. Augustine established.
1598–1630	New Mexico missions established.
1607	English Protestants settle Jamestown.
1608	France establishes Québec.
1619	First Africans arrive in English colonies.
1626	Dutch Reformed establish New Netherland.
1630s	Swedish Lutherans establish New Sweden.
1630–42	Puritan migration to New England.
1634	Catholic Calvert family founds Maryland.
1636	Harvard College established; Roger Williams founds Rhode Island.
1639	Roger Williams founds first Baptist church.
c. 1650–1750	French missions in North America.
1654	First Jews arrive at New Amsterdam.
1656	First Quakers arrive in English colonies.
1658	First Jewish congregation in English colonies founded.
1675–76	King Philip's War destroys John Eliot's "Praying Indian" villages.
1680	Pueblo Revolt, New Mexico.
1681	William Penn establishes Pennsylvania.
1683	German Lutheran, Reformed, and Mennonite migration to Pennsylvania; Germantown founded.
1687	Eusebio Francisco Kino from New Spain to Arizona.
1691	English government requires religious toleration in Massachusetts; Calvert family overthrown in Maryland.
1701	Church of England founds SPG.
1706	Presbytery of Philadelphia formed.
1707	Philadelphia Baptist Association founded.
1717	Synod of Philadelphia formed.
1719	German Brethren arrive in Germantown.
1720s	Early Amish migrations to Pennsylvania.
1730s–60s	Great Awakening.
1739–41	George Whitefield tour.
1732	Ephrata community founded.
1735	First Moravians arrive in English colonies.
1742	German Brethren form annual conference.
1746	Presbyterians establish College of New Jersey (Princeton University).

1748	German Lutherans form Ministerium of Pennsylvania.
1750s	New England Baptists go South.
1755	Acadians expelled from Nova Scotia, establish "cajun" culture in Louisiana
1756	Quakers renounce control of Pennsylvania government.
1760s	Early Methodist societies appear in English colonies.
1763	Pontiac's uprising.
1768	Jesuits evicted from Spanish Empire.
1769	Junípero Serra from New Spain to California.
1769–1823	California missions established.
1776–1809	Shaker communities proliferate.
1780s	Church of England disestablished.
1784	Russian Orthodox arrive at Kodiak Island; Methodist Episcopal Church founded.
1788	Presbyterian Church in the United States of America convenes first General Assembly.
1789	First Catholic diocese in United States established at Baltimore.
1791	First Amendment guarantees religious freedom.
1790s–1830s	Second Great Awakening.
1793	German Reformed Church established.
c. 1800	Handsome Lake's movement.
1801	Cane Ridge revival; Yale revivals; Congregational-Presbyterian "Plan of Union."
1804	Rappites establish Harmony.
1805–12	Tecumseh and the Shawnee Prophet promotes Indian militance in Ohio Valley and Great Lakes.
1810	Cumberland Presbyterian Church established; ABCFM established.
1816	African Methodist Episcopal (AME) Church established.
1818	Opukahaia to New England.
1820	ABCFM missionaries arrive in Hawaii.
1820s–30s	Finney revivals.
1821	African Methodist Episcopal Zion (AMEZ) Church founded.
1825	American Unitarian Association established.
1826	American Home Mission Society founded.
1830	Joseph Smith establishes Church of Jesus Christ of Latter-Day Saints.
1830–60	Ashkenazic Jewish immigration.
1831	Nat Turner rebellion.
1832	Black Hawk's resistance movement; Disciples of Christ established.
1833	Mexican government dissolves California missions; Universalist Church of America founded.
1834	Ivan Veniaminov arrives in Sitka, Alaska.
1836	Transcendental Club formed.

1840	Sitka becomes Russian Orthodox diocese.
1841	Brook Farm formed.
1844	Joseph Smith murdered.
1845	Southern Baptist Convention established; Henry Thoreau to Walden Pond.
1845–60	Irish immigration wave.
1847	Mormons arrive in Utah.
1848	Spiritualism emerges; Oneida community founded.
1850s	Smohalla's movement.
1853	Chinese immigrants establish first Buddhist temple.
1854	Amana colony established.
1867	Russian government sells Alaska to United States; National Camp Meeting Association for the Promotion of Holiness founded.
1870	Colored (later Christian) Methodist Episcopal (CME) founded.
c. 1870	Peyote religion appears in United States; Wodziwob's movement.
1873	Union of American Hebrew Congregations founded.
1875	Theosophical Society founded.
1877	Chief Joseph's Rebellion.
1879	Church of Christ, Scientist established.
1880	Church of God (Anderson, Indiana) founded.
1880–1920	"New" immigration from eastern and southern Europe, Asia, Near East, Middle East.
1882	Legislation restricting Chinese immigration prompts disappearance of Chinese Buddhist temples.
1889	Wovoka develops Ghost Dance; Jodo Shinshu missionaries arrive in Hawaii.
1890	Massacre at Wounded Knee; Mormon church rejects polygamy.
1890s	"New Thought" emerges.
1893	World's Parliament of Religions brings non-Western religions to America; National Spiritualist Association of Churches founded.
1894	Vedanta Society founded; Baha'i faith arrives in United States.
1895	National Baptist Convention (NBC) founded.
1896	Church of God and Saints of Christ founded.
1897	Polish National Catholic Church founded; Church of God in Christ founded.
1898	Union of Orthodox Jewish Congregations in America founded; Jodo Shinshu missionaries arrive in San Francisco.
1899	Buddhist Mission of North America founded.
1901	Pentecostalism emerges.
1905	Russian Orthodox Church transfers diocesan seat to New York City.
1906–09	Azusa Street revival.
1907	Church of God (Cleveland, Tennessee) founded.

1908	Church of the Nazarene founded; Pope declares United States no longer a mission field of Roman Catholic Church.
1909	First Sikh *gurdwara* in the United States established.
1911	Pentecostal Holiness Church founded.
1913	Moorish Holy Temple of Science founded; United Synagogue of America (now United Synagogue of Conservative Judaism) founded.
1914	Assemblies of God founded; United Negro Improvement Association founded.
1919	Commandment Keepers Congregation of the Living God founded; World Christian Fundamentals Association founded.
1920s	Mexican immigration wave.
1920s–30s	Ethnic Eastern Orthodox churches develop.
1921	African Orthodox Church founded.
1922	Greek Archdiocese of North and South America founded; Pilgrim Holiness Church founded.
1925	Self-Realization Fellowship (SRF) founded; Scopes trial.
1929	Nation of Islam founded.
1943	Renewal of Chinese immigration and Chinese Buddhism.
1944	Native American Church established; Buddhist Churches of North America founded.
1949	First Billy Graham crusade held in Los Angeles.
1953	Unification Church founded; Church of Scientology founded.
1959	Unification Church missionaries arrive in United States.
1960	Nichiren Shoshu of America (later Nichiren Shoshu Academy) founded.
1961	San Francisco Zen Center established; Unitarian Universalist Association established.
1965	Malcolm X assassinated.
1965–present	"Recent" immigration from Latin America, Asia, Africa, Middle East.
1966	Students' International Meditation Society founded; International Society for Krishna Consciousness (ISKCON) founded.
1970	Orthodox Church of America (OCA) founded.
1973	Vajradhatu (Tibetan Buddhist) founded.
1980	American Muslim Mission founded.
1985	American Muslim Mission dissolved.
1990	National Catholic Council for Hispanic Ministry founded.
1995	Greek Archdiocese of United States formed; Million Man March.
1997	Family Federation for World Peace and Unification (USA) founded.

Further Reading

Space does not permit a complete list of studies of the many religious groups and movements mentioned in this atlas. Instead, a list of general reference works is offered. Those in the first four categories below identify further reading on specific aspects of American religious history.

Atlases

Gaustad, Edwin S., and Philip L. Barlow. *The New Historical Atlas of Religion in America*. New York: Oxford University Press, 2000.

Encyclopedias

Hirschfelder, Arlene B. *Encyclopedia of Native American Religions*. Revised ed. New York: Facts on File, 2000.

Lippy, Charles L., and Peter W. Williams, eds. *Encyclopedia of the American Religious Experience*. 3 vols. New York: Charles Scribner's Sons, 1988.

Queen, Edward L., II, Stephen R. Prothero, and Gardiner H. Shattuck, Jr. *The Encyclopedia of American Religious History*. 2 vols. New York: Facts on File, 1996.

Melton, J. Gordon. *The Encyclopedia of American Religions*. 6th ed. Detroit, MI: Gale Research, 1999.

Melton, J. Gordon, and James Sauer. *The Encyclopedia of American Religions, Religious Creeds*. 2 vols. Detroit, MI: Gale Research, 1988, 1994.

Murphy, Larry G., J. Gordon Melton, and Gary L. Ward, eds. *Encyclopedia of African-American Religions*. New York: Garland, 1993.

General Narratives and Surveys

Ahlstrom, Sydney E. *A Religious History of the American People*. New Haven: Yale University Press, 1972.

Albanese, Catherine L. *America: Religions and Religion*. 3rd ed. Belmont, CA: Wadsworth, 1999.

Eck, Diana L. *On Common Ground: World Religions in America*. New York: Columbia University Press, 1997.

Gaustad, Edwin S. *A Religious History of America*. Revised ed. San Francisco: Harper and Row, 1990.

Hudson, Winthrop S. *Religion in America*. 4th ed. New York: Macmillan, 1987.

Marsden, George. *Religion and American Culture*. San Diego: Harcourt Brace Jovanovich, 1990.

Miller, Timothy, ed. *America's Alternative Religions*. Albany: State University of New York Press, 1995.

Noll, Mark A. *A History of Christianity in the United States and Canada*. Grand Rapids, MI: W.B. Eerdmans, 1992.

Nuesner, Jacob, ed. *World Religions in America: An Introduction*. Louisville, KY: Westminster/John Knox Press, 1994.

Wentz, Richard E. *Religion in the New World: The Shaping of Religious Traditions in the United States*. Minneapolis: Fortress Press, 1990.

Williams, Peter W. *America's Religions: Traditions and Cultures*. New York: Macmillan, 1990.

Dictionaries

Bowden, Henry Warner. *Dictionary of American Religious Biography*. Westport, CT: Greenwood, 1977.

Melton, J. Gordon. *Biographical Dictionary of American Cult and Sect Leaders*. New York: Garland, 1986.

Reid, Daniel G., et al. *Dictionary of Christianity in America*. Downers Grove, IL: InterVarsity Press, 1990.

Statistics

Bradley, Martin B., Norman M. Green, Jr., Dale E. Jones, Mac Lynn, and Lou McNeil. *Churches and Church Membership in the United States 1990*. Atlanta: Glenmary Research Center, 1992.

Johnson, Douglas W., Paul R. Picard, and Bernard Quinn. *Churches and Church Membership in the United States 1971*. Washington, D.C.: Glenmary Research Center, 1974.

Quinn, Bernard, Herman Anderson, Martin Bradley, Paul Goetting, and Peggy Shriver. *Churches and Church Membership in the United States 1980*. Atlanta: Glenmary Research Center, 1982.

United States Bureau of the Census. *Religious Bodies: 1906*. Washington, D.C.: U.S. Government Printing Office, 1906.

United States Bureau of the Census. *Religious Bodies: 1916*. Washington, D.C.: U.S. Government Printing Office, 1919.

United States Bureau of the Census. *Census of Religious Bodies: 1926*. Washington, D.C.: U.S. Government Printing Office, 1929.

United States Bureau of the Census. *Religious Bodies: 1936*. Washington, D.C.: U.S. Government Printing Office, 1936.

Geographic Perspectives

Maffly-Kipp, Laurie, *Eastward Ho! American Religion from the Perspective of the Pacific Rim*, in Thomas A. Tweed, ed., *Retelling U.S. Religious History*. Berkeley, CA: University of California Press, 1970.

Shortridge, James. *A New Regionalization of American Religion*. Journal for the Scientific Study of Religion 16, June 1977, pp.143–154.

Zelinsky, Wilber. *An Approach to the Religious Geography of the United States: Patterns of Church Membership in 1952*. Annals of the Association of American Geographers 51, June 1961, pp.139–193.

Index

Acknowledgments

This atlas owes its existence to many people. Mark Carnes, general editor of this atlas series, has offered friendly advice on mapping and has been helpful in many ways besides. Editor Kevin Ohe and cartographers Elsa Gibert and Malcolm Swanston have worked closely and—patiently with the author throughout. Peter Williams, David Narrett, and Sam Oppenheim have read portions of the manuscript and must take credit for some of its strengths—though no blame for any of its imperfections. Philip Barlow and Ed Gaustad, both well familiar with the process of mapping American religion, have also been helpful with their suggestions; the latter in particular has been a pioneering and inspirational figure in this area. Also inspirational have been Laurie Maffly-Kipp, who has called for the kind of geographic decentering of America religion scholarship that this atlas attempts, and Diana Eck, whose emphasis on the United States as home to world religions has informed Part Five. The library faculty at California State University, Stanislaus have been ever ready and willing to help from the inception of this book, never seeming to mind being deluged with questions and interlibrary loan orders.

Several other people deserve special mention for their help with various phases and aspects of this atlas. They are:

Jo Antonson, Historical Society of Alaska
Ken Bowers, National Teaching Office, Baha'i National Center
Orienne Denslow, Sitka Historical Society / Isabel Miller Museum
Richard Francaviglia, University of Texas at Arlington
Kit Goodwin, University of Texas at Arlington
Mandi Johnson, Georgia Historical Society
Eric Komori, Hawaii State Historic Preservation Division
Arthur J. Krim
Jerald T. Milanich, University of Florida
Debbie Newman, Arizona Historical Society
Mohamed Nimer, Council on American Islamic Relations
Lucinda Glenn Rand, Graduate Theological Union
Philip Schanker, Family Federation for World Peace and Unity USA
Barbara S. Smith
Robert Stockman, DePaul University
Helen Tanner, Newberry Library
Mark Turdo, Moravian Historical Society
Richard White, Stanford University
Mary Wyant, Map and Geographic Information Center, University of New Mexico
Rev. Stephen Yale, Graduate Theological Union

Most important are the three people mentioned in the dedication. My father, Gilbert Carroll, early encouraged my love of maps and atlases, but is not here to see this book. My mother, Judith Moskowitz, always a source of strength and support, will doubtless view this atlas with his eyes as well as her own. My wife, Iris Carroll, has patiently and lovingly witnessed the atlas-making process at far closer range than either of them. My debt to all three is far greater than words can express.

Last, I think that the same page listing illustration credits should include a few map credits as well, as follows:

Quakerism map and colonial religious regions maps are adapted from *The New Historical Atlas of Religion in America* (New York: Oxford University Press, 2000) Philip L. Barlow and Edwin S. Gaustad.

African missions map: adapted from Walter L. Williams, *Black Americans and the Evangelization of Africa* (Madison: University of Wisconsin Press, 1982), xviii.

Data for the map on page 103 was provided by the Council on American Islamic Relations, Washington, D.C.

Current religious regions map: Adapted from Wilbur Zelinsky, *An Approach to the Religious Geography of the United States: Patterns of Church Membership in 1952*, Annals of the Association of American Geographers 51, June 1961: pp.139–193.

Pictures are reproduced by permission of, or have been provided by the following:

Arcadia Editions Limited: p. 22
Author: p. 106
Mary Evans Picture Library: p. 36
New York Public Library, Astor Lennox and Tilden Foundation: p. 40
Santa Barbara Mission Archive Library: p.23
Southwest Museum, Los Angeles: p. 16
State Historical Society of Wisconsin, Madison/Abertype Collection: p. 99
Private Collections: pp. 12, 13, 27, 30, 44, 49, 55, 58, 68, 70, 82, 84, 90, 94, 112, 113, 125

Design: Elsa Gibert, Malcolm Swanston.

Cartography: Elsa Gibert, with Jeanne Radford, and Malcolm Swanston.